REDISCOVERING THE EUCHARIST

RAYMOND MOLONEY SJ

First published in 2012 by Messenger Publications

Messenger Publications,
37 Lower Leeson Street, Dublin 2
www.messenger.ie

Printed in Ireland

ISBN 978-1-872245-85-0

Designed by Messenger Publications Design Department
Typeset in Optima and Trajan Pro

MESSENGER
PUBLICATIONS
JESUITS in IRELAND

CONTENTS

FOREWORD

The Eucharist remains the greatest treasure of the Church. As a result there is no end to the writings of people on this subject, and no limit to the depths of mystery and meaning waiting to be discovered by the faithful in the heart of the sacrament. In this little book you will find some short reflections on various aspects of the Eucharist. Most of these chapters appeared originally as a series of articles in *The Irish Messenger of the Sacred Heart*. The order of the chapters follows loosely the structure of the Mass, as the Table of Contents shows, but the purpose here is not to set out a systematic treatment of our doctrine on Mass and sacrament. That is something available in many other publications, including a book by this author, *The Splendour of the Eucharist* (Dublin: Veritas, 2003), still available. The purpose here is rather simply to set out a series of short independent chapters on various topics, each chapter giving the reader a few thoughts on a single aspect of this great mystery. The whole book is small enough to be read from cover to cover in a few sessions, but that is not really the purpose in mind. Each chapter stands on its own, and should provide matter for a few brief moments of personal prayer or reflection. One or two chapters at a time should be just enough to give one's thoughts some focus as one retires to one's room to pray or when one comes before the Blessed Sacrament for a moment's peace and quiet The occasion for this publication is the International Eucharistic Congress, Dublin, 2012, and it may be found a helpful book for individual and group preparation for that event; but its usefulness will extend beyond that date, since the topics it reflects on are part of the timeless inheritance of the Christian faith and of the ongoing life of the Church.

PART 1:
GOING TO MASS

☙ 1 ❧
THE CHURCH'S WORSHIP

"Mass is so boring!" How often parents have been hearing that complaint from their children in recent years! Behind such a remark can lie the unspoken question, "What do I get out of the Mass?" Here in the first of our reflections on the Mass we need to see just how false this question is. The Mass is not about "I" but about "we". It is something we do only in the Church and as part of the Church. By "Church" here I am not referring to the building at the centre of the parish. I am referring to the People of God, the Body of Christ, a world-wide community bound together in a mysterious union of faith and worship. The Mass is that Church at prayer and worship.

The Mass is not something one does thinking only of oneself and of one's personal obligation before God. Such an attitude would be clean contrary to the meaning of the Mass. The Mass is all about others and our relationship with others. We come to Mass as part of the People of God. We are summoned to Mass by God because we are part of his people, and ever since the Old Testament he has summoned people to worship him on the Sabbath day. However since the New Testament it goes even deeper than that.

When we Christians come together for Mass we are the People of God, the Body of Christ in this place. This is something greater than just you and me and our next-door neighbours saying their prayers. We are playing our part in something that the Church is doing for the world, and then there is a grace and power at work amongst us which is greater that just the sum of our individual prayers. On any Sunday we could pray at home, listening to Mass on the radio or on television. Of course, if we are sick or indisposed, that is a good thing to do, but if we are in good health, it is no substitute for going to Mass ourselves and being part of the Church at worship. As members of the congregation we tap into that special power and energy which circulates in the Body of Christ. Where the people of God are gathered in Christ's name, that is where the Holy Spirit is for us. That is what we tap into. There is no substitute for that

The Mass is not just about me. It is about other people as well. How often those who complain about the Mass being boring are thinking only of themselves and of what they can get out of it! Let them begin to think rather of other people and of how they are helped by what we do at Mass. Just as the Church is there to help us by its grace and prayer, so we are there to help other people, to help the Church. We pray for our families, our parish, our country and the Church throughout the world. The Mass is a matter of my responsibility for others, offering my life to God for other people, for all those whom I love. It is not primarily about what they or the Church can do for me. The Mass is about what we can do for other people and what we can do for the Church and for the world.

2
CELEBRATING A WAY OF LIFE

One of the most profound things Our Lord ever said about how we are to live is his teaching, "Anyone who wants to save his life will lose it, but anyone who loses his life for my sake will find it" (Mt 16:25). At first that sounds rather obscure, but in fact it is very concrete.

"Losing life" means being unselfish. It means being forgetful of self for the sake of other people and ultimately for the sake of God. As regards "finding life", have you ever noticed that unselfish people have got something. They have an inner strength and peace and joy which the rest of us often miss. They have found something here below which is a beginning of the life they will have for ever with God in heaven.

This teaching of Our Lord puts in a nutshell nothing less than the inner meaning of Christian love. Here he is summing up for us the whole way of life he wishes us to lead as Christians, and notice that it comes in two movements, losing life to find life. I stress these two movements. We are going to find them in another way when we come to apply all this to the Mass, for the Mass is a celebration of the way of life which our Lord has set before us.

To celebrate a way of life in ritual is a common experience. One will recall how in Red Square in Moscow every November Russian communism used to celebrate a way of life based on military power and centralized control. In Britain, when the monarch opens parliament, the occasion is a celebration of a way of life in which tradition and privilege play a major role. In a somewhat parallel way the ritual of the Eucharist celebrates the way of life and the values of life which our Lord has set before us.

TWO MOVEMENTS

Just as there are these two movements in the meaning of Christian love, so there are two movements to be found when that way of life comes to be celebrated in the rituals of the Mass. The Eucharist can be viewed under two main aspects: it is sacrifice and it is banquet. The sacrifice is expressed especially in the solemn act of worship we offer to God during the Eucharistic Prayer. The banquet is expressed especially at the table of holy communion. The sacrifice brings home to us how our Lord lost his life in our service. The banquet brings home to us how he found life for himself and for us by rising from the dead and feasting with his disciples (Acts 10:41). In this way the Eucharist is the celebration of the death and resurrection of the Lord, the supreme instance of someone losing life to find life.

Celebrating our way of life together helps us not only to express but to deepen the values that hold us together. The banquet expresses the joy and fulfilment which the life of faith means for us, but the sacrifice reminds us that the gateway to the resurrection is the cross. The path of the Eucharist is through sacrifice to banquet; it is in giving that we receive; it is in losing life that we find life. Not only does the celebration refresh our memories and bring those values of self-sacrifice and love of neighbour before us, but it also gives us the opportunity to commit ourselves once again to those values and so to continue the struggle to make them more real in our lives and to serve our brothers and sisters in Christ for his sake.

≈ 3 ≈
THE FAMILY AT MASS

It is sometimes said that our generation is a "me first" generation. This cynical remark ignores an awful lot of good things happening in our world: the labours of so many people for the deprived and under-privileged, our concern for the Third World. If there is a grain of truth in the remark, it has something to do with the way people today are so conscious of being individuals, and maybe too often the individual comes first. Frank Sinatra spoke for a whole generation when he sang, "I did it my way!"

One area where this issue can raise its ugly head is in family life today, particularly as parents and children begin to feel divided by the generation gap. Not only do teenagers often find it difficult to talk to their parents and share interests with them, but many even find it difficult to sit down at table and eat a meal together. Young people often prefer to heat up a pizza and eat it before the television rather than to sit down at the family table for good solid meat and vegetables.

This same difficulty reaches into the world of prayer and worship. Long ago it was a common sight to see a whole family go to Sunday

Mass together. For many families that is now a thing of the past. The changes in the Mass have meant different styles of liturgy for different age-groups. In some ways this is a good thing if it helps to keep young people going to Mass, but it weakens the old saying that the family that prays together stays together.

THE DOMESTIC CHURCH

The Mass is all about other people and our living with other people in the various communities to which we belong. Of these, the first and most important Christian community is the family. It is where we first experience the meaning of life in the Church, and so the Vatican Council called the Christian family "the domestic church" (*Lumen gentium*, 11). As a result, recent Popes have been concerned to hold before us as an ideal the custom that all the members of a particular family should try, where possible, to go to Mass together on a Sunday. The Eucharist is the means we have from Christ for binding us to one another in love and mutual forgiveness, and those are qualities which every family need.

Where that ideal is not possible or practicable, one always remains a member of one's family. That means that, whether we are in their company or not, we should always carry the whole family in our heart. We pray for them. We offer ourselves to God for them. The closer we are to God, the more we can help our family before God. If we refuse to go to Mass, that takes something from the whole family as well as from ourselves. For a Christian being a member of a Christian family is part of being a member of Christ's body, and in that body we are all members one of another (Rom 12:5). Being a member of a Christian family is not only a privilege and a benefit; it is also a responsibility. We do not live life simply on our own. We are all bound up with one another, for good or for ill.

4
SUNDAY AND RESURRECTION

From the earliest years of Christian faith Sunday and Eucharist have gone together – the Day of the Lord for the banquet of the Lord. The link between the two is the fact of the resurrection. Sunday is special from the beginning because it was the day on which Christ rose from the dead. Vatican II described it as "the original feast-day". It was the feast of the resurrection even before Easter became the annual celebration of that mystery.

For Jews the weekly day for special worship was, and still is, Saturday, the weekly Sabbath. From early on Christians marked their distinction from Jews by gathering for worship on Sundays. One of the early martyrs realised this when he wrote, "Those who used to live according to the ancient order of things have come to a new hope; they no longer observe the (Jewish) Sabbath but rather the Lord's day" – St Ignatius of Antioch (+ c. 110).

THE SACRIFICE OF THE RESURRECTION

The main way for celebrating the resurrection in the Christian Church is the Eucharist. If our Lord's story had ended with his death, we would not be celebrating him at all. The Eucharist celebrates the Lord's death and resurrection as one, for the resurrection is the manifestation of the victory which our Lord had already won on the cross. The Christ of the Eucharist is the victorious risen Christ bringing us the fruits of the sacrifice he first offered in his death and resurrection. That is why one of the great Fathers of the Church, St. Gregory Nazianzen, can refer to the Eucharist as "the sacrifice of the resurrection".

A DAY OF JOY

If Sunday is the day of the resurrection, it is to be a day of joy. When we begin to find our Sunday Mass a burden, then something is wrong. An ancient writer in third century Syria went so far as to say – perhaps too strongly – "On the day of the Lord be always joyful, for he who is sad on the Lord's Day commits a sin." The Mass on Sunday is a way of affirming that life has meaning and that our struggles have value before God. If Christ is risen, we shall one day rise also and be united with those we love in a way beyond all imagining. The Eucharist is our food to help us on that journey, the only journey that really matters in the long run.

A FAMILY DAY

Sunday should also be a day of freedom from work. That was taught by Vatican II also. It is a way of getting out from under the burden of everyday and affirming that there is more to life than the daily round of work and routine. A simple way of doing that is to make Sunday a family day - a day of doing things with the family, eating together, playing together and if possible going to Mass together as a family. We can apply to Sunday what a Jewish writer wrote of the Sabbath: on that day the father of the family is king, the mother is queen and all the children are royalty too.

A DAY FOR OTHERS

Then Sunday is a day for thinking of others – and that is something central to the meaning of the Eucharist. Mass is always something we offer for others as well as for ourselves. First of all we think of our own families, remembering the old saying that the family that prays together stays together. Then we include in our intentions our friends, our country, those struggling with illness, alcohol and drugs, those working for Christ in the Third World. But our concern for others can be practical too. We could, for instance, go visiting people, grandparents, the sick, the forgotten. Christians are called to be "people for others". That too is part of the meaning of the Eucharist and of why our Lord came back to us after the resurrection.

THE FIGHT FOR SUNDAY

Truly Sunday is one of the Lord's gifts to us. Not only is there the honour he bestows on us by inviting us to his table but there is also that providence of his which has promoted Sunday as a day of joy and of freedom from work. Unfortunately this gift from the Lord is under threat in the modern world. The general atmosphere of indifference and secularism makes people forgetful of the true meaning of life, which is what Sunday is all about. There is also the threat from the consumer society which puts pressure on shops to open for business, curtailing the freedom of their workers and by that fact making it more difficult for them to find time to worship. Indeed in many of our towns Sunday is scarcely distinguishable from any other day. Pope Benedict has spoken of "the fight for Sunday", calling on Christians to be conscious of the need for a special effort to resist the forces of modern life and to restore the Sunday as one of the great signs that man does not live by bread alone.

PART 2:
ENTERING INTO MASS

⚬ 5 ⚬
MUSIC AND SONG AT MASS

The scene is Croke Park, summer 2009. The event is the Dublin concert of Bono and U2 as part of their world tour. People come not only from every corner of Ireland but from other countries and continents as well. The drawing-power of Irish music is truly amazing, and it is not only contemporary music that causes ripples. Even our older songs and airs have a world-wide appeal. Music and song are things we do well. We sing at concerts, at football matches, on bar-stools, but not in church!

MUSIC AT VATICAN II
Why is it that our singing in church is so often half-hearted and uninspiring? Maybe we are just not convinced enough that it really matters. If that is true, then we are certainly out of line with the mind of the Church as expressed at Vatican II and on various occasions since.

The council opened their discussion of music and song in the liturgy with the following resounding statement: "The musical tradition of the universal Church is a treasure of incomparable value, outstanding among other artistic expressions, not least because the combination of sacred song and words makes an indispensable and integral contribution to solemn liturgy." The council Fathers devoted so much attention to the topic because this issue touched on some of the main points they wanted to make about liturgy generally, especially the need to promote active participation of all in the liturgy as an aid to deepening our sense of community.

ACTIVE PARTICIPATION

An adequate account of remedies for the situation would take us too far afield. Here we will just consider a few. If active participation is as important as Vatican II tells us, then a primary concern has to be getting as many people as possible to take part. Beautiful motets by choirs in the choir-loft are not the answer. The songs chosen should be those which people enjoy singing, and they must have available the words they are asked to sing. It is a help if there is someone with a good voice to lead them from a microphone. The choice of music must be adapted to the congregation. For instance, where young people predominate, it must be their kind of music. However, the main thing is that we have a deep conviction that it all really matters. Nothing less will rouse us out of our lethargy.

The Church has some fine things to say that might help convince us. Music, says the Vatican Council, can add a sense of splendour and solemnity to the liturgy, bringing home to people in a non-verbal way the wonder and significance of our worship. It helps to make prayer more pleasing and to promote unity of minds and hearts. Singing is one of the signs of joy in our hearts, and singing as a group means that the joy is something that binds us together. The Church recalls St Augustine who wrote that singing is a mark of the lover, and it quotes an old saying that singing our prayers is to pray twice over. Finally, if we still think that we can do perfectly well without singing at Mass, then it is no harm to bear in mind that our Lord and the apostles joined in song at the Last Supper, as the gospels tell us (Mk 14:26).

6
ALL ARE PRIESTS

Questions concerning ordination to the priesthood frequently make the headlines in the media, but all the talk about these topics could easily make one forget that there is a deeper and more fundamental meaning of priesthood which belongs to the laity as well. It is what we mean by phrases like "the priesthood of all the faithful" or "the priesthood of the baptized". It is something carefully distinguished by the Church from the priesthood of the ordained, though both forms of priesthood have in common that they flow from the priesthood of Christ.

A PRIESTLY PEOPLE
The central idea behind the priesthood of the baptized is the fact that priests are mediators. They are called to mediate divine life and grace to other people. That is their privilege and responsibility, and this is a role which is laid on every Christian by their Baptism and expressed again in Confirmation. Baptism makes us members of the People of God, but this people is a priestly people (1 Pet 2:5); this means that they have the task of passing on to the world the life and grace they have received from Christ.

This is why, in the sacraments of Baptism and Confirmation, the new Christians are anointed with the Oil of Chrism. This oil is a special scented oil, blessed by the bishop on Holy Thursday, for the use of the diocese in the coming year. It is the same oil as that used in the ordination of priests. The point is that all these sacramental graces are a share in Christ's own priesthood, which was first revealed to the Church on the first Holy Thursday at the Last Supper.

MEMBERS OF ONE ANOTHER
When the Second Vatican Council came to speak of the active participation of all the faithful in the liturgy of the Church it invoked the priesthood of the baptized as the basis of their role and dignity (*Liturgy Constitution* 14). An active role in the liturgy certainly

manifests that priesthood, but this priesthood is something broader than that. It really points to a dignity and power that belong to every good act and prayer of the believer, within the liturgy or elsewhere.

No man is an island, said the poet. As Christians we are never alone, but always belong to one another in a mysterious way. Every good work of ours, every prayer, every act of kindness, can become a fragrant offering before Almighty God for the benefit of those for whom we pray. I am a channel of grace to them as they are a channel of grace to me. That is what it means to be mediators to one another. As St. Paul said, we are all members, one of another (Rom 12:5).

PRIESTS FOR OTHERS

Behind this plan of things stands Our Lord himself, the High Priest of all our prayers and offerings. He is the first one who mediates the grace of God to the world, but in his goodness he has chosen to share that role with all the baptized. This sharing in his role is part of our belonging to his mystical body, and the special place for celebrating our union with that body is the Eucharist. This role that he gives us should inspire us at Mass to pray for other people and to offer ourselves in union with Christ for all those, living and dead, who depend on us before God. We are priests for others at all times, but especially during the Mass.

≈ 7 ≈

FORGIVENESS

Forgiveness is one of the most difficult things our Lord asked us to do, yet there is no doubt but that it is central to being a Christian. In the dark years of the recent troubles in Northern Ireland, among the few chinks of light have been some outstanding acts of forgiveness on the part of people who had lost loved ones or who had been treated with gross injustice by the State. I remember in particular a young Belfast working-man who lost his whole youth in prison for an offence he did not commit. He later told how after years of hating those responsible he came to see that such hatred destroys no one as much as oneself, and that, even while still wrongfully imprisoned, his only future lay in forgiveness.

Now Christianity is all about forgiveness. Baptism makes us Christians, and Baptism is all about God's forgiving the world. If we are truly to receive God's forgiveness ourselves, we must accept the challenge to become forgiving persons in our own lives also. That point is put before us by our Lord himself in a number of places in the gospel, not least in the Our Father: Forgive us our trespasses as we forgive those who trespass against us. That prayer will cover the ordinary set-backs of life easily enough, but there are times when the difficulty of being truly forgiving makes us wonder whether we can really say the Our Father at all.

If we have been seriously hurt by those we love and respect, the wound will be all the deeper. Indeed we may be unable to cope with the pain and anger at first and may have to be content just to let time calm down our anger and to let that forgiving grace grow gradually within us. If a crime has been committed against you or others, the law should take its course, but forgiveness remains an issue for the person no matter what happens in the public course of things. It is about letting time and grace heal the anger within yourself; otherwise it will eat away within you and destroy your peace.

FORGIVENESS INCLUDES THE CHURCH

The issue becomes all the more difficult when you feel that it is the Church itself which has let you down in the person of one of its representatives. The first instinct of people in that situation is anger at the whole Church and a determination to have nothing more to do with it. However we might recall the piece of ancient wisdom which warns against making major decisions when in an emotional state. Indeed it makes no sense at such a time to turn one's back on the Church, for part of what we need in that situation is precisely the grace to overcome that destroying anger within us and to be open to forgiveness; and one of the main sources of that grace is precisely the Church and its sacraments, especially the Eucharist

Here we have to come back to what our Christian faith teaches us. The Church is not just an organisation which we might join or leave as the mood takes us. The Church is a mystery of faith. It is so much bigger that any individual within it. The Church is the bark of Peter who himself needed forgiveness; it is the People of God, the Body of Christ. Despite the shortcomings of individual members, it is the place where God has laid up the graces we need. We might think of all this at the beginning of every Mass when we say the "I Confess" together. We do not come to Mass as the just ones who do not need a Saviour (Mk 2:17). We come as imperfect human beings bearing the common burden of our sinfulness and needing one another's forgiveness as we need the forgiveness of God; and remember, one of those saying the "I Confess" is the priest.

❧ 8 ❧
WORD AND SACRAMENT

Before the Vatican Council people used to be more conscious of the obligation of going to Mass on Sunday. We used to talk of "getting" Mass; and to fulfil your obligation properly you had to be there at least from the gospel on. The Mass was often seen as just a block of rituals, without much sense of how it all fits together in a meaningful way.

The Vatican Council was breaking away from that kind of thinking when it taught us that the Mass is made up of two main parts, the Liturgy of the Word and the Liturgy of the Eucharist. In this way, as in many others, it was pointing out that the ritual has an inner meaning. It is not just a question of one thing after another. Each part has its own meaning and function, and one part helps the other. Elsewhere the council taught us that Bible Services on their own are a good thing in themselves, so that raises the question of why it is appropriate that the Liturgy of the Word and the Liturgy of the Eucharist should go together. The reason can be put simply: the Eucharist needs the word and the word needs the Eucharist.

19

THE EUCHARIST NEEDS THE WORD

All the sacraments, including the Eucharist, are sacraments of faith. That means that sacraments do not bear fruit apart from our faith. They are not magic. They do not act automatically by carrying out certain prayers and gestures. They need the living faith of those who receive them if they are to bring about what Christ wants of them.

Indeed, the more open we are to God's grace, and the more generous we are before him, the deeper and more lasting will be the effect of the sacrament for us. Now faith, says the Vatican Council, is born of the word and nourished by the word; and that is precisely the role of the Liturgy of the Word. It is there to deepen our faith and make us more open to God so that our celebration of the Eucharist will be all the more fruitful in our lives.

THE WORD NEEDS THE EUCHARIST

I mentioned above that the Vatican Council encouraged the custom of Bible Services on certain occasions. Though these services are not followed immediately by the Eucharist, they normally take place among Christians who have given the Eucharist its due place in their lives. Catholics generally have a profound conviction that they cannot live their lives as Christians without the Eucharist. This is the basic reason why the Liturgy of the Eucharist follows the Liturgy of the Word in the Mass.

The word of God on its own is not enough. We see that most clearly in the way the story of the apostles developed. For three years they listened to the word of God from the greatest teacher the world has ever heard; they experienced the greatest friendship the world has ever known; but at the end of it all they abandoned him, and Christ died alone.

The Christian Church never really got under way until Christ came back from the grave in the power of his death and resurrection. Only then did they have the special strength and grace won for them by Our Lord's dying and rising; and this mystery of his death and resurrection is the heart of the Eucharist where it continues to nourish the life of the Church, enabling us to live up to the challenges put before us in the Lord's ministry of the word.

PREPARATION OF THE GIFTS

In every Mass, when the Readings, the homily and the Prayers of the Faithful are over, there comes a quiet time as the celebrant sets out the bread and wine on the altar. This part of the Mass is called the Preparation of the Gifts. It is a time with its own message for us that we could easily miss, and it is one which we need to understand better in order to turn it into prayer, rather than letting the mind wander in distractions between the collection and the Preface.

This section of the Mass is the one where the greatest changes were made after Vatican II. The Church wanted to make it clear that the keynote of this part of the liturgy is *preparation*. It is not the case that we first offer bread and wine on their own, as it were, in the kind of offering of bread and wine and other fruits of the earth which we find in many religions. Many people used to think of this part of the Mass in that way, but this was precisely the view which the Church wanted to set aside, and so it changed this part of the Mass so thoroughly. What is offered in the Mass is the one offering of the New Law, our Lord's body and blood, into which our gifts have been changed. That is the one and only offering in the Mass. The prayer to express it is the Eucharistic Prayer, and consequently the section of the Mass before the Eucharistic Prayer is not a time of offering but of preparation for the offering.

JEWISH TABLE CUSTOMS

As a model for the liturgy of this section of the Mass the Vatican II reformers turned to the customs of the Jews on the occasion of a festive meal such as the Last Supper. In a Jewish festive meal, before the solemn table blessings with which the meal was formally opened, there were some preliminary rituals of blessing. The prayers we now use when the priest receives the bread and wine are like those preliminary blessings of the Jews, their opening words taken straight from the ancient Jewish tradition of prayer: "Blessed are you, Lord God of all creation..."

Drawing on Jewish prayer in this way fits in with the presence of other Jewish influences on this part of the Mass. For instance there is the custom of the priest washing his hands. This is part of how the Jews prepared for a banquet. Simple as this gesture is, it reminds us of meals in the gospel, for instance the purification jars at Cana and the Lord's washing of the apostles' feet at the Last Supper. Yet a further Jewish gesture is the addition of water to the wine. This was always the way with the Jews, perhaps only for practical reasons, because their wine was rather thick, but for Christians it is always seen as a precious symbol of how our offering of ourselves is to be mingled with the offering of Christ and lose itself in his. The presence of these Jewish customs is a striking reminder to us of the continuous link between our worship and the world of our Lord and the apostles.

PRAYING THE RITUAL

If preparation is the keynote of these rituals, it must also be the keynote of our prayer at this section of the Mass. As the bread and wine are being prepared for the great mystery of change and offering at the Eucharistic Prayer, we must prepare ourselves for this same offering. As we watch the preparations on the altar, we place ourselves, our lives and our hearts on the paten and in the cup. Often in the course of a day or week, we wander off the right path, but now we want to signify our desire to get back on track, reasserting that God is the basic meaning of our lives. We want to renew our commitment to him and give our lives to him for ourselves, our families and for all whom we love. That is what we do at this point of the Mass.

PART 3:
THE EUCHARISTIC SACRIFICE

～ 10 ～
A CHRISTIAN PASSOVER

Why does Easter come every year sometime after the spring equinox? The reason is not far to seek. Easter grew out of the Jewish Passover and ever since its beginning in Egypt the Passover has been celebrated at this time of the year. The Passover is one of the greatest feasts in the Jewish calendar. It is the annual celebration of the events we call the Exodus. Those events marked the great wonder by which God intervened on behalf of the Jewish people; he rescued them from the slavery of Egypt and brought them off on the great trek through the desert towards the Promised Land.

All the first Christians were Jews, and even as Christians they continued to celebrate the Passover, but now calling to mind the events with which our Lord celebrated his last Passover on earth. However it was not just a question of fond memories of the past. They were conscious that the great sacrifice with which our Lord's life on earth came to an end was in fact the fulfilment of what the Jewish Passover was all about. By his death Christ rescued us from the slavery of sin. By his resurrection he brought the Promised Land within our reach; and by his Last Supper he gave us all this in mystery through the liturgy of the Eucharist.

The Fourth Gospel

Christians have long seen the Eucharist as a kind of Christian Passover. This follows from the way John's gospel presents Christ's death and resurrection as the great Passover sacrifice for the salvation of the world. John had already described our Lord as "the Lamb of God", and on the cross his body was treated in exactly the way the Jews treated a paschal lamb: his death took place at the very hour when the Passover victims were being offered in the temple (Jn 19:4); not a bone was broken in him and his heart was pierced (Jn 19:33f). The Jews did not break the bones of the paschal victims but they pierced their hearts.

At the Last Supper our Lord had anticipated his sacrifice by giving it a central place in the new meaning he was giving to the paschal bread and cup. The words he used over them showed that he was thinking of his passion – "body given" and "blood poured out" – and so, in this way, through the bread and cup of the blessing, he was taking on himself the great sacrifice that lay before him, the sacrifice which would bring that blessing to fulfilment.

Flesh and Blood

It fits in with this way of thinking of his death that the gifts we receive in the Eucharist are referred to in John's gospel in Passover language. On the night the Passover was established in Egypt, the Jews were told to take the "flesh" and "blood" of the Passover victim to save them from the doom that hung over the country (Exod 12:7). In the sixth chapter of John's gospel the same language is used for the food that gives us life, his flesh and blood. In the Western Church ever since the middle ages, in order to underline that link, the bread we bring to the Eucharist is unleavened bread, since that is the kind of bread which the Jews used for the Passover, as they still do.

In our Christian Passover, which is the Eucharist, we receive the flesh and blood of our paschal victim, the great Paschal Lamb. In receiving his sacramental flesh and blood we do not contain Christ; Christ contains us. Our Paschal Lamb is so much greater than we are. In a sense he is the whole Church, head and members; and we, in consuming his sacramental flesh and blood, are drawn into that greater reality which is Christ's great Passover sacrifice for the salvation of the world.

The village of Oberammergau in Bavaria is known throughout the world for its famous passion-play. This event, which is staged only once every ten years, re-enacts the story of our Lord's passion in all its details. One performance can take up to eight hours to complete. Passion-plays were a common feature of life in the middle ages, but the one in Oberammergau is the main one to survive in our time in a regular way.

THE MASS AS A PASSION-PLAY

In the middle ages the people often thought of the Mass as a kind of drama or passion-play. At that time, of course, the Mass was in Latin, but very few people understood that language. As a result they could not follow the meaning of the various prayers, and they had no missals to provide a translation, such as we used to have before the vernacular was introduced.

Thinking of the Mass as a kind of passion-play gave them a way of relating to what was going on in the sanctuary, even though it meant interpreting gestures in the Mass in ways that had nothing to do with their real meaning. For example, at the priest's washing of his hands at the offertory they thought of Pilate washing his hands before sending our Lord to his death. At the great silence after the consecration during the Eucharistic Prayer they thought of the silence of the three days of our Lord in the tomb.

We have always said that the Mass is the same sacrifice as that of the cross and that this sacrifice is made present to us in the Mass. As a result it might be held that, in a sense, the people following the Mass as a kind of passion-play were in tune with one of the central truths about the mystery. While this is true up to a point, their approach is also misleading, for it does not do justice to the resurrection. The

Mass does not repeat or mime the sacrifice of Calvary in that literal way. Christ does not suffer or die in the Mass. Having died once, Christ dies now no more (cfr Heb 9:22).

THE KERNEL OF THE MYSTERY

What is made present in the Mass is the kernel of what happened in Christ's death and resurrection, namely his great self-offering in love for the salvation of the world. What saved us on the cross was not so much the sufferings which Christ bore as the love with which he bore them. It was that love which made up for the sins of the world and became the source of the new life of grace which burst upon the world on the morning of the resurrection.

At the same time it is possible for us to learn something from the medieval practice. The structure of the Mass can be seen to follow in a very loose way the main lines of Christ's work of redemption, though that was not the original intention. The liturgy of the word corresponds to the time of preparation in Old and New Testaments, with the gospel reading making present events in Christ's life.

While Christ's death and resurrection are present to us throughout the liturgy of the Eucharist, it is appropriate to think especially of Christ's self-offering on the cross during the great prayer of offering which is the Eucharistic Prayer. Then the banquet of holy communion follows. It recalls to us especially the joy and victory of the Lord's resurrection, particularly as associated with those unforgettable meals which he ate with them after he rose from the dead (Acts 10:41). The life, death and resurrection of the Lord are the source of salvation for the world, and in every Mass that life, death and resurrection are made present to us again when we celebrate them in faith.

≈ 12 ≈
THE EUCHARIST AND THE CROSS

Once I was saying Mass in an impoverished suburb of Nairobi, Kenya, a parish in the care of the Jesuits. The church was a poor corrugated-iron affair, and we were only gradually getting proper furnishing in place. Shortly before that Sunday we had installed a fine crucifix behind the altar.

As I was beginning the Mass, a young boy, quite unselfconsciously, came up and stood in front of the altar, transfixed by the crucifix. Clearly he had never seen anything like it before. We are so used to the crucifix having a prominent place at the altar that we no longer see what an extraordinary thing it is in itself, and how even more extraordinary it is to place such an image of torture and death at the centre of our celebration of life. From another point of view, however, given all that we believe about the cross in our lives, surely that is where it belongs.

THE MASS AS SACRIFICE

We speak of the Mass as a sacrifice, but in this day and age we hardly know what sacrifice means. In the western world we have no experience of ritual offering apart from the Mass. Some people have even gone so far as to say that, whatever the truth of the term in earlier ages of the Church, it no longer seems helpful for modern preaching about the Mass. However this criticism has not got very far. People have realised that not only does the notion run deep in the tradition of the Church, it comes out of the very heart of the Christian faith.

The central message of Christian faith is not just about life after death but about life *through* death. The Lord tells us that we must take up the cross every day in all the trials of life, great and small, for the gateway to the resurrection is the cross. It is through learning to die with him in all the hardships of life that we will win through to rising with him when the time of final salvation comes.

At the centre of every Eucharist stands the cross. If our Lord's self-sacrifice on the cross is so central to the ordinary living of Christianity, it has to be central in our worship as well. At the Last Supper our Lord joined the mystery of his self-sacrifice to the outward forms of bread and wine so that his sacrifice might become the nourishment and strengthening of our efforts to follow after him on the royal road of the cross.

EXPLAINING THE SACRIFICE

As a result it cannot be a question of getting rid of the term "sacrifice" but of learning to explain it in such a way as to make the link between the self-offering of Christ in every Mass and the offering we make of ourselves as we try to live our lives according to the pattern he has set before us. As the Lord himself said, "It is in losing life that we find life" (Mt 16:25). It is in accepting the crosses of life in a spirit of self-sacrifice that we unite ourselves for ever with our suffering and risen Saviour.

What then of my young African friend in the parish in Nairobi? He taught me a lesson that morning not to take the cross for granted. It must be one of those things hidden from the learned which is revealed to little ones.

⚘ 13 ⚘
THE HOUR OF JESUS

Every so often we come across people whose lives have been lived in obscurity until one day they are caught up in some striking event that creates a sensation. For a brief period they are celebrities, photographed, interviewed and spoken of far and wide. It might be some sports achievement, some literary award or sadly some crime. Commonly after the hue and cry die down; some "celebrities" return to their previous obscurity, though for others their fame is never forgotten. That moment in the limelight will always be their "hour".

AN HOUR OF VICTORY

In the fourth gospel we find our Lord talking of his hour. We first hear of it at Cana where he gives as his reason why he is slow to act that "my hour has not yet come" (Jn 2:4). This hour is spoken of no less than eight times in the course of this gospel. Twice we are told that the hostility against our Lord is held back because that hour has not yet come (Jn 7:30; 8:20). Then at the Last Supper we learn that the hour has finally come (Jn 13:1). It is an hour in which the

Son of Man will be glorified by the Father (Jn 12:23; 17:1) but only in the mysterious ways of God's plan. His glorification comes only when he is raised up on the cross. This hour is his moment of victory when he overcomes the forces of evil on the cross; but the key to this moment is revealed in Christ's great Eucharistic Prayer at the Last Supper when he offers himself to the Father out of love (Jn 17:1ff).

A TIMELESS HOUR

The hour of Jesus is something more than a moment of fame. It is the moment of redemption. At that point the mysterious plan of God comes to a head in bringing about the salvation of all who are to be saved, from the dawn of history to the end of the world. It is as if, in that hour, time stands still. As one great student of the bible put it, this hour is presented in such a way in the fourth gospel that it rises above the flow of events in a kind of permanence outside time (Ignace de la Potterie).

Though Jesus' hour is centred on the cross, there is a sense in which the Last Supper enters into it (Jn 17:1), and indeed every Eucharist enters into it. This is one indication from the New Testament why we should believe that the sacrifice of Christ is made present in every Mass. The Mass belongs to this mysterious and timeless hour of Jesus; in it the work of our redemption is carried out and the permanent fruits of his dying and rising flow into the world.

AN HOUR OF GLORY

We are reminded of this truth by that presence of a crucifix on the altar which the preceding chapter referred to. The crucifix is the sign of all that happens in Christ's hour. However it is not only a question of recalling the sufferings of Christ on the cross. Christ's hour is the point at which he rises above his sufferings and offers them to his Father in love.

As a result it is the sign of that victory which is eventually made manifest in the resurrection. In that sense the resurrection begins on the cross and the crucified Christ is Christ unconquered. On the cross, as the fourth gospel puts it, Christ is glorified (Jn 12:23; 17:1), and to the eyes of faith his hour is an hour of glory.

～ 14 ～
THE GREAT PRAYER

At the centre of every Mass there is the Eucharistic Prayer, also called the canon of the Mass. It begins with the brief dialogue between priest and people before the preface and reaches its conclusion with the solemn act of praise, "Through him, and with him, and in him…" to which the people respond with the great Amen. Most of us are familiar with the four main Eucharistic Prayers which are found in every missal, but there are also further official texts available, some in an appendix to the new missal.

Among all the acts of worship which go to make up the Mass this is the principal one, and sometimes for that reason it is called "the Great Prayer". The main point however which makes this prayer so special is that it is much more that just a prayer, much more than just a form of words to God. It is action. It is an act of worship that draws us into the central action of the Mass. On the surface it looks like just our local act of worship, but on closer reading we will see that it is an act of worship by the whole Church of God, and ultimately the act of worship by Christ himself which he first carried out on the cross and now perpetuates on our behalf in heaven.

However running through the various texts there are three basic movements of prayer into which we must enter if we are to make this prayer our own. They are thanksgiving to the Father, commemoration of the Son and petition for the grace of the Holy Spirit. We will now consider each of these in turn.

THANKSGIVING

Every Eucharistic Prayer opens with praise and thanksgiving to the Father. It is like the way the Our Father opens with the hallowing of God's name (Mt 6:9). There are many things for which we can thank God in the Mass, but at this stage of the celebration we are thanking him especially for the great gift of redemption.

The prefaces of the liturgy colour the prayer according to the season by picking out particular aspects of that redemption which the

Church wishes to commemorate, but underlying all these aspects is the fundamental gift which the Father has given us, namely his very own Son. As the fourth gospel puts it, "God so loved the world that he gave his only Son" (Jn 3:16). That is the fundamental reason why the Church bursts out in praise as we sing or say, "Holy, Holy, Holy Lord God of hosts." This acclamation is a most striking expression of the unity of heaven and earth in the worship of God through Christ.

COMMEMORATIVE OFFERING

This recall of God's gift of his Son leads naturally to a commemoration of what the Son did for our salvation, and this history reaches its high-point in the two events which are proclaimed as one at the centre of every Eucharistic Prayer when the words of our Lord at the Last Supper are invoked. Christ's death is commemorated when we hear of "his body given", "his blood poured out". His resurrection is proclaimed when the priest speaks of a new covenant and the forgiveness of sins, for these show that his death was victorious. The death and resurrection of Jesus form the heart of every Mass, for not only are they called to mind in the way we have described, but, as the Church teaches, these mysterious events are made present in every Eucharist.

However we would miss the whole point of this commemoration if we did not appreciate that all this is not just something happening on the altar. In the faith of the Church it is a commemorative offering, that is to say that we do not truly commemorate Christ's self-offering in his death and resurrection unless we offer ourselves to the Father through, with and in our Saviour.

PETITION

The work of the Son in his dying and rising flows into the work of the Holy Spirit which the risen Lord sends us "to complete his work on earth" – as the Fourth Eucharistic Prayer puts it, or as the new translation puts it, "bringing to perfection his work in the world". Certainly we will need the strengthening of the Holy Spirit if our Eucharist is to be fruitful within us in the way the Lord desires.

The various fruits of the Eucharist all come together in that gift of love and unity among our fellow human beings without which our love of God will never be true (1 Jn 4:20). In every Eucharistic Prayer this concern for unity takes the form of intercession for various groups in the Church. Indeed we can see these petitions as expressions of an underlying prayer for the building up of the Church. The Second Eucharistic Prayer puts it very clearly in the familiar translation: "May all of us be brought together in unity by the Holy Spirit."

CONCLUSION

These three themes, praise, commemoration and petition, are, as we said, the basic movements of worship in the Church's great prayer at the centre of the Mass. These are the themes which we must learn to make our own so that, when we come to the end of the prayer, we may truly say Amen to all that has gone before.

～ 15 ～
THE SACRAFICIAL SPIRIT

In most of the religions of the world people spontaneously express their feelings before God in some form of sacrificial ritual. They know instinctively what their ritual means, though they might not be able to put it into words. In the western world we have lost that sense, and so we have to spell out what exactly passes in the hearts of human beings when they come to sacrifice. What we are talking about is the sacrificial spirit, and generally it refers to four main movements of the human heart.

ADORATION

The first and most fundamental desire of the sacrificial spirit is to adore God. In this movement within us we bow down before the wonder of the God who made us; we acknowledge that he is our Lord and Maker, and that to him we owe everything. As a consequence we desire to give ourselves to God and to surrender all that we have and are to him. Alfred Delp, a German Jesuit who was executed by the Nazis for his resistance to their system, once wrote: "Adoration is the road that leads man to himself."

PRAISE AND THANKSGIVING

The desire to adore God moves easily into a desire to praise and thank him for all his goodness to us. In this way we wish to express outwardly what we feel within us before God. We praise God because of what he is in himself, the loving Father of the universe and the source of all the wonders of heaven and earth. We thank him because of all the good things which he has showered upon us, especially for all the love we have received in the Christian family, which is for us the best image of the love with which God wants to surround us for ever in heaven,

PETITION

We have so many needs in life, it is only to be expected that God wants to meet those needs, but he likes to do that in answer to our prayers. This makes our prayer all the more personal and human, even though he knows what we need before we ask him (Mt 6:8). The earnestness of our petitions has always been one of the key motives in offering sacrifice to God.

ATONEMENT

One of the main petitions that people bring before God in sacrifice is for forgiveness and mercy for ourselves and for others. By such a desire we go some way towards making up for the sins, great and small, which come between us and God. Despite how much God deserves our love and loyalty, human weakness is a fact of life. Since this weakness leads us into such offence against the goodness of God, the least we can do is to acknowledge that fact and ask for grace to overcome our sins. By atonement (also called propitiation) we seek to outweigh the offensiveness of our sins by the grace-given sincerity of our desire to return to God and to recover what we have lost by our sins.

In listing these various aspects of the sacrificial spirit we are not suggesting that our Lord ever spelt them out in this explicit detail. Here we are simply setting out in an ordered way the kind of notions which the people of our Lord's time would have associated with the sacrificial tradition. Sacrifice is a way of expressing through ritual those thoughts and feelings which cannot easily be put into words.

When our Lord spoke of Christian worship in a sacrificial way, he was implying that the Eucharist would take over from the ancient Temple the expression of the sacrificial spirit with which they were familiar. In this way he was indicating that when the ancient forms of sacrifice associated with the Jewish Temple would have passed away, it was still important that these deep needs and instincts of the human heart would find expression in the new form of worship he was leaving us.

～ 16 ～
THANKING GOD

Joe is a young Irishman in his 20's. He is a graduate in information technology and a child of the Celtic Tiger. He knows all about computers and is employed in a successful firm. His parents are religious, but Joe rarely darkens the door of the church. Not that he is hostile to the faith, but ever since his late teens there always seemed to be more interesting things to do.

In previous generations in Ireland, when times were hard and money was in short supply, people generally had little hesitation about going to Mass on Sunday, no matter to what age-group they belonged. It is striking about young people today that so many of them have so much to thank God for, particularly in contrast to the hardships of earlier generations, yet the thought of all they owe to God never seems to cross their minds in any formal way.

THANKSGIVING IS HUMAN

To say "thank you" is one of the most human things we do. It is an obligation that arises from something deep within us, and to fail to

34

do so is to fail in common humanity. As William Barclay, the great Presbyterian scholar, put it, "We are all in debt to life. We came into it at the peril of someone else's life, and we would never have survived without the care of those who loved us."

The best model for our debt of gratitude to God is our debt of gratitude to our parents, but what we owe them for our upbringing and for the gift of life itself is a pale reflection of what we owe to almighty God, not only for the gift of life but for the way he keeps us in being and lavishes on us, from moment to moment, the many good things that we enjoy. There is nothing too small or incidental in our lives but that it can be seen as coming to us from the hand of God (Mt 10:29-31).

THANKSGIVING AND EUCHARIST

Thanksgiving is at the heart of the Mass, for the term *eucharist* comes from the Greek word for thanksgiving. One of the special intentions of every Mass is to give God praise and thanksgiving for the countless gifts he showers upon us from day to day and week to week. This intention is expressed in the Mass at certain moments in particular, such as at the "Glory to God in the highest", at the Preface leading up to the "Holy, Holy, Holy" and at the climax of the Eucharistic Prayer at the "Through him, and with him, and in him"; but in a sense it runs through the whole Mass even when it is not explicit, for the whole Mass is one solemn public act of worship, praise and thanksgiving through Christ "through whom you give us everything that is good".

This debt of gratitude to God gives us a way of thinking of our obligation to go to Mass on Sunday. That obligation is not just something that comes from man-made law. It is an obligation that arises from what we are as human beings, owing everything we have and are to almighty God.

We can express our thanks to God in various ways, for instance in moments of private prayer and at grace before and after meals. Our Sunday Mass, however, is the way given us by Christ and his Church to fulfil our obligation in a solemn and public way, for only such a repeated and formal way of doing so seems adequate to express the depth of all we owe to God every day of the week, every moment of our lives. To fail to do so is nothing to be casual about. It is, as we said, a failure in common humanity. St Ignatius Loyola once put it strongly: "Considered in comparison with the divine bounty, ingratitude is, of all evils imaginable, one of the things most abominable in the eyes of our Creator and Lord."

17
THE FAITHFUL DEPARTED

For the ancient Celts the year was divided into two main periods, the time of darkness and the time of light. The time of darkness began with the great feast of *Samhain* on November 1st, while that of light began on May 1st. With the lessening of the light, people withdrew from their summer activities of grazing and harvesting and so had more time to reflect on life and in particular on the other world. Our feasts of All Saints and All Souls fit in with this mood, and indeed some scholars believe that these feasts had an Irish origin. Be that as it may, at this time of year, as we see the death of vegetation and the falling of the leaves, it is natural to reflect on our own mortality and on those who have gone before us into another world.

The Christian background of these feast-days is the doctrine of the communion of saints, one of the most consoling truths in our faith. It is not just a question of union with those who wear their halos as canonized saints. It is about all of us, whether great saints or little sinners, as long as we are friends of God, for we are all bound together in the mysterious ways of the Body of Christ.

PRAYING FOR OUR LOVED ONES

This truth is especially important when we come to celebrate the Eucharist. It is expressed with special clarity in the first of the four main Eucharistic Prayers of the Church, the one we call the Roman Canon. There we clearly come before God in union not only with the Church on earth from the Pope down, but truly in union with the whole Church, in heaven and on earth and under the earth. By those "under the earth" we refer to the faithful departed, whose bodies await the resurrection in cemetery or tomb. Their special day is the feast of All Souls, but their memory remains with us in our thoughts and prayers throughout the year.

We are familiar with praying for our loved ones who have passed on, but we not only pray for them; we pray through them and with them, whether they are in Purgatory or in heaven. One of the most consoling truths about the Eucharist is that nowhere else are we as close to our dead as at the Mass. It is the one place where we can still do something *with* them. Together with them we can honour almighty God and pray for our families, our country and our world.

AN ANCIENT ROMAN PRAYER

All this is expressed in a moving way in the ancient Eucharistic Prayer of the Roman Church. The key thought running through this entire prayer is one of communion with the various ranks of people mentioned in the prayer. In the case of the saints in heaven we pray not only with them but through them. We pray for and with all the leaders of the Church on earth, and we pray for and with our faithful departed ones.

This is done especially at that part of the Eucharistic Prayer which is called the Memento of the Dead in words filled with poignancy and compassion. We will conclude our reflections with these ancient phrases, translating them more literally than in the official version:

Remember, Lord, those who have gone before us with the sign of faith and sleep in the sleep of peace, especially those for whom we now pray. Grant, we pray you, to them and to all who rest in Christ, a place of restoration, light and peace through Christ our Lord: Amen.

PART 4:
THE GREAT BANQUET

❧ 18 ❧
THE OUR FATHER IN THE MASS

Between the Eucharistic Prayer and holy communion comes the Our Father. It is a kind of link between the two, or like a clasp holding together the two ends of a necklace. Among the various parts of the Eucharist, the main ones are these two. The Eucharistic Prayer is the central act of offering in the Mass, making present to us Christ's great act of self-offering on the cross. Holy communion is the great banquet where we celebrate Christ's resurrection and look forward to that "feast in the kingdom of heaven" promised us by the Lord (Mt 8:11). In between we have the Our Father. At once it sums up the main lines of the Eucharistic Prayer and, at the same time, looks forward to the kingdom of heaven, which we anticipate in holy communion.

AFTER THE EUCHARISTIC PRAYER
In giving us the Our Father, our Lord was giving us not only a formula of prayer but a style of prayer, We find this style of his not only in our Lord's own great priestly prayer at the Last Supper (Jn 17) but also in our Eucharistic Prayers. In all of them God is spoken of

as the Father, and they all begin with the worship of that Father in praise and thanksgiving: "Hallowed be thy name". These prayers are prayed in the first person plural, because we Christians are never alone; we pray only as members of the Body of Christ, praying for others as they pray for us.

The key words of prayer in the Our Father, which link up with Christ's self-offering on the cross, come in the petition, "Thy will be done on earth as it is in heaven." We remember the words of our Lord in Gethsemane, "Not my will but thine be done" (Mk 14:36). In this way he showed us something of what was in his heart at that moment, namely the self-offering, which was to carry him through the grim events of the following day, right up to his final cry, "Father, into thy hands I commend my spirit" (Lk 23:46). Such self-offering is the key to all prayer and worship, and that is why our Lord put it at the centre of the Our Father; and so now it comes in this key moment of the Mass, enabling us to express our personal Yes to that renewal of Christ's self-offering which the Church has just presented to the Father in the Eucharistic Prayer.

BEFORE THE COMMUNION

The Our Father comes in the Mass just as we move from sacrifice to banquet, from cross to resurrection. When the liturgy thinks of the resurrection, it speaks of the coming of God's kingdom, and that begins for us in the Our Father: "Thy kingdom come." From there we go on to pray, "…for the kingdom, the power and the glory are yours…" At holy communion we are called to the Lord's Supper, the Supper of the Lamb, which in scripture is one of the images of the wedding-feast in the kingdom of heaven (Apoc 19:9).

The early Christians thought of the Our Father as a prayer of preparation for the kingdom. In that spirit they prayed the final petitions of the prayer, which sum up fundamental conditions which the Lord has laid upon us about entry into the kingdom: we must renew our forgiveness of others; we must strengthen our resistance to temptation; we must re-commit ourselves to relying, not on our own powers, but on the protecting mercy of God to save us from all evil. These are the graces we need when it comes to "standing before the Son of Man" (Lk 21:36), whether in receiving holy communion or at the last judgment.

～ 19 ～
THE BREAKING OF BREAD

One of the most striking, yet simple, rituals in the course of the Mass is that of the breaking of bread. It comes as part of the preparation for holy communion, following on the Our Father and the sign of peace. It is a gesture which goes right back to the way the Jews of our Lord's day – as they still do – celebrated the brief ritual of the praise of God with which every meal began, a custom which corresponds to our grace before meals.

While blessing God for his gifts the father of the Jewish family breaks the bread in order to share it with the other family members. This expresses their union in the one family as they share in the one loaf. It is surely full of meaning that it was to this ritual of union in the one loaf that our Lord turned at the Last Supper when he began the institution of the Eucharist (cf St Paul in 1 Cor 10:17).

THE MEAL IN THE DESERT
The gesture of breaking reminds us of some well-known events in the gospel story. We think, first of all, of those occasions when our Lord multiplied the loaves and fishes for the hungry multitude (Mk 6:30-44; 8:1-10). By that miracle he was preparing the people for the Eucharist, and it is remarkable how his actions on those occasions are the same as those which we later find in the Mass.

In this way he was preparing us for the greater miracle of multiplication in the sacrament. In each host he multiplies the mystery of his presence and has hidden a message there for each of us. No matter how many come to receive holy communion, he loves each one of us and he gives himself totally to each one as he once did in another way on the cross.

The Meal at Emmaus

Another memory that comes to mind is the unforgettable scene in the inn at Emmaus (Lk 24:13-35). The two disciples sit down at table with their guest. They have been so impressed by his words along the road that they invite him to say grace.

There must be something in the way that he does this, whether recalling how he has done it at the Last Supper or how he used to do it in their missionary travels together: they recognise him at once in the breaking of the bread, and then he disappears from their sight. All that is left of him is the broken bread lying on the table. In this way he is telling them that in future they cannot rely on the visibility of his presence. What they will have instead will be the bread of the sacrament received from the table of the Eucharist.

The Ritual Meaning

Indeed there is a sense in which the whole Eucharistic mystery is summed up in this simple ritual of the Mass. The action is in two parts; we break in order to share. Sharing in the sacrament is a way of sharing in the life of the Lord's resurrection. But there is no sharing without the breaking, and that breaking reminds us of our Lord's body broken on the cross. There is no sharing in the resurrection without first passing through the mystery of the cross. There is no banquet without the sacrifice. It is in giving that we receive. It is in dying to self that we are reborn to eternal life.

∽ 20 ∾
Loaves And Fishes

One unforgettable day was that day when our Lord fed thousands of people with five loaves and two fish. After the whole day out in the open with them the disciples wanted to send the people off so that they could buy food on the journey home. Our Lord had other plans. He got his helpers to arrange them all in groups on the green grass, and then he took the only food they had, the famous five loaves and two fish. Holding a loaf in one hand and a fish in the other, he raised his eyes to heaven and began to pray. That is the way every Jewish meal begins, but in this case he was already going through the ritual which one day would be fulfilled in his celebration of the Eucharist.

In his prayer our Lord blessed and thanked his Father for the gift of food, he prayed for all those present, and so he began to break the food into pieces and handed it to the waiting disciples. They began to bring it down among the groups on the grass, but to their astonishment, the more they came back for, the more there was to give. The bread and fish just kept multiplying in his hands until all had been fed. Then the disciples filled their baskets with the leftovers, and all went home. It was a day they never forgot.

THE MEANING OF THE SIGN

It was only with the passage of time that the full meaning of what had happened gradually dawned on them. The first lesson it taught them was that Jesus was the great prophet promised by Moses (Deut 18:15); indeed on that day Jesus himself was seen as a new Moses, feeding his people in the desert as Moses had done when manna fell from heaven (Exod 16:15).

But there was an even deeper message in those events which only became clearer much later. In time the Church began to see that in working this extraordinary miracle our Lord was preparing them for the mystery of the Eucharist. Part of the wonder of this sacrament is the way our Lord multiplies his presence in every host throughout the world. That too is part of what was being foreshadowed on that evening long ago.

But that is not all. More wonderful even than the multiplication of his presence is the multiplication of his love. The one is the proof of the other. The multiplication of the loaves is a mystery because it reveals one of the great secrets of Christ's love. In ordinary human love there is a limit: the more widely it spreads the less intense it tends to be. But that is not the way when one is loved by an infinite love.

Christ loves all of us, but he loves each of us with his total love as though there were no one else to love and no one else to die for. That is one reason why Christ multiplies his presence totally in each and every host, so that in giving us the host he is giving himself totally to each one. It is his way of saying, I love you; I died for you; I now give myself totally to you as I once gave myself totally for you upon the cross. Greater love no one has than that one lays down one's life for one's friends (Jn 15:13). Each of us is such a friend. The host proves it.

ᵥ 21 ᵥ
PEACE

"Peace I leave with you, my peace I give to you. Not as the world gives do I give to you. Let not your hearts be troubled, nor let them be afraid" (Jn 14:27). Our Lord spoke these memorable words to the apostles at the Last Supper. Already Judas had gone to betray him and the powers of darkness were closing in, but still he could talk of peace and of not being afraid. Clearly the peace he spoke of was not peace as this world understands it. He spoke rather of that inner peace which is the gift of God and flows from friendship with God.

By speaking in this way at the Last Supper our Lord was joining the gift of this peace with the gift of the Eucharist. It is one of the great graces of the Eucharist, like love, unity and the presence of the Holy Spirit – all of which he spoke about as he celebrated the sacrament on that solemn night. Worldly peace is sought by *getting*, by piling up riches and security. Christ's peace comes by *giving*, by love and unselfishness, according to the example of Christ's own life. Such peace is the fruit of the Holy Spirit (Rom 14:17), something that surpasses all merely human understanding (Phil 4:7).

THE SIGN OF PEACE
With this teaching of Christ in the background we can see why the liturgy has given us the rite of peace in the Mass. We should notice that it comes shortly after our prayer for forgiveness and reconciliation in the Our Father. It is introduced by the beautiful prayer for Christ's peace, "Lord Jesus Christ, who said to your apostles, peace I leave

you, my peace I give you..." It is then expressed in a simple gesture, as when we shake hands with one another.

The ritual has taken various forms over the centuries, but the shaking of hands seems to suit our particular culture. In the context of the Mass the gesture has a special meaning since it is a way of extending the symbolism of the sacrament itself. It not only expresses the union that we already have with other people but it also has something of the power of a sacramental, deepening our peace and reconciliation, not only with those whose hands we shake, but with the whole people of God. In some liturgies the sign of peace comes at the end of the liturgy of the word, but in western liturgies, ever since ancient times, it has been celebrated at this point of the Mass as part of the immediate preparation for holy communion.

CHRIST IS OUR PEACE

Often the person we greet is a complete stranger, but that does not matter. We are all members of one another in the body of Christ, and as St. Paul says, it is because we are all gathered into the one body that the peace of Christ reigns in our hearts (Col 3:15). When the person we greet is someone we know, the gesture will be an expression of love and regard, but sometimes there can be in it a sense of reconciliation as well. Where family-members come to Mass together, the ritual has a special significance as expressing and deepening the sacred unity of the Christian family.

Here we might learn something from St Augustine, who sees the peace we already have from Christ in this life as a preparation for that peace which we will have in another world. "As our Lord is about to go, he leaves peace with us. When he will come at the end of time, he will give peace to us. He leaves peace with us in this age; he will give peace to us in the age to come. He leaves peace with us that even here we may love one another; there he will give us his peace, where all discord will be at an end... Now as he ascends from us – while not withdrawing from us – what does he leave us except himself? For he himself is our peace, who has brought into unity that which had fallen apart."

TRANSFIGURATION

The day our Lord asked Peter, James and John to come up the mountain with him, the three apostles can scarcely have guessed what they were going to see. Probably they just thought that it was our Lord following his usual custom of seeking out a place apart in which to pray. At prayer our Lord always looked somewhat different, but this time the difference was quite extraordinary. Suddenly the inner mystery of our Lord flashed out before their eyes in all its brilliance. His divinity shone out through his body, his face dazzled like the sun, and the two great visionaries of the Old Testament, Moses and Elijah, took their place reverently at his side.

This mystery of the Lord's transfiguration is celebrated twice in the course of the year, once on the Second Sunday of Lent and once on August 6th. When it comes in Lent, it is overshadowed somewhat by the thought of the Passion, for which our Lord was preparing his disciples by this miracle. When it comes in August, we can celebrate more clearly the glory of the Lord and respond to what the mystery tells us about our own ultimate destiny.

TRANSFIGURATION IN THE EUCHARIST
This event has also got something to say about the Eucharist. Before the eyes of the apostles Christ was physically changed, revealing something of the divine power within him to change things and, as St. Paul puts it, to "subdue all things unto himself" (Phil 3:21). The Eucharist is about change also, especially as bread and wine are changed into Christ's body and blood. This is what we call "transubstantiation". In the ancient Church they did not yet have that word, but some of the ancient writers used instead the word "transfiguration" for what is basically the same truth. In the Eucharist there is a "transfiguration" of bread and wine into Christ's body and blood.

In that same passage from his letter to the Philippians St. Paul speaks of yet another sense of transfiguration. He refers to the change of everything, including our bodies and souls, in the general resurrection at the end of time. An epistle of Peter has it that there will be "new heavens and a new earth" (2 Pet 3:13). So we have three kinds of transfiguration: that on the mountain, that at the end of time in the resurrection of the dead, and that in the miracle of every Eucharist. They are all connected, firstly, because they are all about change; secondly, because one comes about with a view to the other. On the mountain Christ revealed that he has the power to change the world. At the end of time he will change everything, ourselves included, alive or dead, so that there will be new heavens and a new earth.

CHANGING THE WORLD

In order for us to reach that final victory we have to be changed, and so it is in order to change us that Christ changes our bread and wine in the Eucharist, so that we can go out to help change the world. Of themselves bread and wine cannot change us in the way our Lord desires; that is why they have to be changed. Only Christ's body and blood can change us in the way he has in mind. They are part of that new heavens and new earth into which Christ is changing everything. By the power of Christ in them to subdue all things, the host and the cup of the sacrament can help that process of change in us, so that one day we may rise with Christ in the transfiguration of all things at the end of time.

≫ 23 ≪
CORPUS CHRISTI ~ THE BODY OF CHRIST

The Eucharist is the Church's greatest treasure because it contains Christ himself who is the total wealth of our faith and our love. Catholics love the Eucharist. It is the great secret love at the heart of the Catholic faith which outsiders never really understand – a love so deep that we can hardly put it into words. We manifest it from the beginning in all the excitement around First Holy Communion, and then there are the processions, benediction, exposition and the annual celebration of Corpus Christi – the feast of our Lord's body and blood.

In former centuries the state and the established church of the time did their best to wrest the Catholics of Ireland from this belief, but – marvel of marvel – the vast majority held on, despite dungeon, fire and sword, for this was a treasure which they received from God himself. Though they might be deprived of all their worldly possessions, and even of life itself, they clung on through thick and thin to the only treasure left to them. Fidelity to the Mass was the immediate occasion of the arrest and execution of the beatified Irish martyrs Maurice McKenraghty, John Kearney OFM and William Tiery OSA, but there were many others, known and unknown.

A GREAT FAMINE

But now a great tragedy has struck us down. The tragedy is that of famine. By that I refer not to the potato famine of the nineteenth century, nor to the great famines of the twentieth century – Ukraine, Ethiopia, North Korea – but to a twenty first century famine that is happening all around us. Despite all the graces and consolations that our people have received from the Eucharist in the past, many of our contemporaries have turned their backs on Mass and sacrament and no longer celebrate them; and that leads to a great famine just as surely as if there were no bread and potatoes to feed us.

When there is no food to feed us, it soon becomes obvious – staring eyes, pot-bellied youngsters, breasts run dry. One of the problems with the Eucharistic famine is that usually nothing seems to have changed externally in the individuals who have fallen away. There are some signs, but to see them you have to consider the society as a whole. There the signs are only too obvious: the increase in greed, in bitterness, in marital infidelity, in fornication and in the collapse of family life among so many today. These things were always there to some extent, but they have now reached the point where they are just accepted as part of modern living.

THE BREAD OF LIFE

The sixth chapter of John's gospel makes clear the link between the Eucharist and the life of grace. The sacrament is the Bread of Life. That means that it is to nourish within us the life of grace and of fidelity to God. Just as we need food to nourish our physical lives, so we need this Bread of Life to nourish our moral and spiritual lives. Without me, says the Lord at the Last Supper, you can do nothing (Jn 15:5).

Here too we can see the point of the mystery of transubstantiation. Bread and wine will nourish our natural lives, but to nourish the life of grace, the divine life within us, the bread and wine must be changed into something else, namely into the body, blood, soul and divinity of Jesus Christ, who alone has the power to make us truly grow in love and become what God wants us to be. Those who eat my flesh and drink my blood, says the Lord, have eternal life and I will raise them up on the last day (Jn 6:54).

～❧ 24 ❧～
SIGN OF HIS SACRIFICE

We are familiar with the words we hear every time we go to communion, as the priest presents host or chalice to us, The Body of Christ, The Blood of Christ. This simple ritual has a long history, going back to the very early centuries. When the faithful reply with their "Amen", the ritual is an expression of the faith of the recipients in the reality of the sacrament. Over time, devotion led people to add on various phrases, expanding the original brief words in order to express the meaning more clearly. An ancient Coptic missal is a good example: the minister says, "This is truly the body and blood of Emmanuel our God," to which the believer replies, "Amen. I believe."

In the middle ages, particularly after communion was no longer distributed into the hand of the believer, a shift of meaning took place and the words became a formula of blessing without any reply from the faithful. Older people might recall the long Latin formula used in the old liturgy by the priest with each communicant: "May the body of our Lord Jesus Christ preserve your soul for everlasting life, Amen." (*Corpus Domini nostri Jesu Christi custodiat animam tuam in vitam aeternam, Amen.*) It was surely a welcome change when, after the Second Vatican Council, the Church returned to the simple words used in early times and instead of the blessing from the priest restored the ancient custom of a mutual sharing of faith between minister and communicant.

THE BODY AND THE BLOOD

There is however a possible misunderstanding that one must guard against if one takes the present words too literally. We have always been taught that in each and every host we have the presence of the whole Christ, body, blood, soul and divinity, as he is now in heaven. The same is true for everyone receiving from the chalice. That is why we can have full communion when we receive under only one species, whether host or chalice. Why then does the Church seem to divide the Lord by speaking only of his body over the host, and only of his blood over the chalice?

The reason is a profound one that leads us into appreciating the sign under which we receive. Though indeed Christ is whole and entire, body, blood, soul and divinity, in heaven – and that is the way we receive him in either species – in holy communion we receive him *under the sign of his death*. In death Christ's body and blood were divided as he poured out for our sakes the last drop of blood in his body. His death was the great work of his love, and in the Eucharist we receive that love, even though Christ now dies no more and is victorious in heaven.

In the host we receive the whole Christ, body, blood, soul and divinity, but under the special sign of his body. In the chalice we receive the whole Christ, body, blood, soul and divinity, but under the special sign of his blood. The two species together are a joint sign of his sacrifice. As a joint sign they remind us of how Christ loved us "unto the end" (Jn 13:1). Going to communion therefore is a sacrificial act. Its meaning is communion in Christ's sacrifice; and it expresses our solemn commitment to respond to Christ's love by living our lives in a sacrificial way, in the love and service of God and of our fellow human beings.

25
THE BREAD OF HEAVEN

In recent years cookery programmes have become very popular on television. You might have followed the one with the title, *You Are What You Eat*. This title sums up a growing awareness among people about the importance of diet. Our health generally has been greatly improved by this growing appreciation of the effect of various foods on heart problems, cholesterol problems and such like. Indeed this has to be one of the factors in enabling people on average to live longer than was formerly the case. Food changes us, and something of the properties of healthy food passes into those who consume it.

Our Lord has given us the sacrament of the altar under the sign of nourishment. This means that the way the sign works on our bodies tells us something about the way the sacrament works on our souls. The Eucharist changes us if we are open to being changed, and something of the unique power and holiness of our Lord himself passes into us.

THE FATHERS OF THE CHURCH
Thoughts along these lines were very much appreciated by those great saints of early times, the Fathers of the Church. St. Gregory of Nyssa (335–94) says of the Eucharist, "The bread that was changed into that body (the body of the Lord) was changed into a divine power." That great saint of the Egyptian church, St. Cyril of Alexandria (378–444) saw the union of the divinity with Christ's humanity in the Incarnation as the source of the life-giving power of his body.

Applying this principle to the sacrament Cyril writes, "Just as one might take a spark and place it in a pile of chaff to keep the seed of fire alight, so Our Lord Jesus, through his own flesh, has hidden his life within us and left it there, as the seed of immortality, to do away with all the corruption that is within us." In a flight of fancy the eighth century Irish poet, Blathmac, wrote, "Happy are they who have Christ as their cook!"

In the Church of the West one of our great teachers was St Augustine (354–430). He saw that the divine Christ is so much greater than any one of us that the ordinary image of taking food should be turned around. He saw Christ speaking to each of us as follows, "You shall not change me into you but you will be changed into me." Pope St Leo I (400–461) seems to have the same idea in mind when he writes that in holy communion "we pass over into that which we consume." We are what we eat!

Growing Like God

We well might wonder what all these mysterious phrases mean in practice. Perhaps we can put it this way. One of the effects of going frequently to communion is that our Lord helps us to grow more like him. Gradually over time the sacrament helps to change us. It is not a change we are going to be able to measure from week to week or even from year to year. Like all profound change it takes time, a long time. Maybe in the later years of a life nourished by the Eucharist – more usually in someone else than in oneself – you will see how a person has become more wise in the ways of God, more tolerant of others, more sympathetic to failure and less ready to condemn. That is one way in which the slow work of Christ, preparing us for another world, will give some sign of its presence and power.

❧ 26 ☙
A Visit From A Friend

Many times in the gospel story we read of our Lord coming to visit people in their homes, often to join them at table. This happened to all kinds of people, good and bad, rich and poor, friends and enemies. Truly, our Lord is "no respecter of persons" (Acts 10:34). The salvation he brings is offered to each and every human being. Of particular interest, however, are the passages where he comes to visit his friends, for there we see how the mutual regard between our Lord and his friends brings joy and blessing to all in that house.

THE FAMILY AT BETHANY

Perhaps the best known example is that of our Lord coming to the family at Bethany, Martha, Mary and Lazarus. He seems to have known them so well that he and his disciples often came to stay with them. The family at Bethany were well off and could afford to put them up. The joy of his friends in having him amongst them is reflected in the costly ointment which Mary poured over his feet, foreshadowing his burial (Jn 12:7). But our Lord can never be outdone in generosity. That is shown by the wonder he worked in raising Lazarus from the dead, foreshadowing the resurrection (Jn 11:1-44).

THE HOUSE OF ZACCHAEUS

Then there is the moving story of Zacchaeus (Lk 19:1-10). Zacchaeus was a low-sized man and, in that society, a despised one, for he got rich out of the taxes of the people. Our Lord, however, saw the potential for good in him. "Hurry, because this day I am to stay in your house." Zacchaeus welcomed him and prepared a feast for him. He renounced his life of exploiting people, and to this our Lord responded with the assurance of forgiveness and salvation. "Today salvation has come to this house."

THE ROOF OF THE CENTURION

Every time we come to holy communion this practice of our Lord is remembered. The story of the centurion is another case of our Lord coming to someone's home, and the Church recalls it by using the words of the old pagan to express our unworthiness: "Lord, I am not worthy that you should enter under my roof" (Lk 7:6f) – words thankfully restored to us in the new translation of the missal . The centurion felt unworthy that our Lord should cross his threshold, but we can assume that our Saviour was not put off, no more than he is put off when we fall down before him.

CÉAD MÍLE FÁILTE ROMHAT, A ÍOSA.
With the eyes of faith the Church sees holy communion as a way in which we are like Martha and Zacchaeus and the centurion. Often the liturgy applies to holy communion the moving words of the last book the bible: "Behold I stand at the door and knock. If anyone hears my voice and opens the door to me, I will come in to him and sup with him and he with me" (Apoc 3:20). All unworthy as we are, we welcome our Saviour "under our roof". Every time we go to communion, our Lord is saying to us as he said to Zacchaeus, "This day I am to stay in your house." Like Martha and the others, we do our best truly to welcome him and to make him feel at home. We spend time with him, talking to him, heart to heart, telling him our troubles, asking his advice and sometimes, like Mary of Bethany, just quietly listening to what he has to say.

❧ 27 ❧
MEMBERS OF HIS BODY

In the preceding chapter of this book we reflected on the meaning of going to holy communion. We saw that in the sacrament we come to our Lord as a friend to a friend, for he is coming to visit us as he once came "under the roof" of the centurion in St. Luke's gospel (Lk 7:1-10). There is, however, yet another way of understanding it, which is also implicit in the words of the Church. In the Third Eucharistic Prayer the Church sees the Eucharist helping us to become "one body" in Christ. We do not think enough of this aspect by which the Eucharist is building up the Body of Christ which is the Church itself. In holy communion we come to our Lord not only as friend to Friend but also as members to the Head.

CHRIST LIVES ON

When our Lord ascended into heaven, the story of his work on earth was only beginning. At that point he assured us that he would always be with us "to the end of time" (Mt 28:20). He continues his work in the world, but now he does it while remaining himself invisible and known only to faith.

But from another point of view he remains visible, namely visible through us, the members of his body. We are the hands and feet of Christ through which he still lives on in the world, going about doing good, promoting his kingdom and helping us to deal with the problems of life. That is the wonderful truth of the mystical body and the communion of saints; and the energy that keeps it going is the energy that we draw from the flesh and blood of Christ in the Eucharist.

St. Paul has a helpful remark that we can apply to the Eucharist. "No man hates his own body but he feeds it and cares for it, as Christ does for the Church, for we are members of his body" (Ephes 5:29f). Holy communion is Christ feeding his body the Church. It is like that scene at the lakeside in John's gospel where our Lord gathered a group of hungry fishermen around a fire that he had made for them, and he fed them with bread and fish (Jn 21:13). It is the same with us in holy communion – the Head nourishing the members of his body, and something of the life and energy of the Head passes into us.

MEN AND WOMEN FOR OTHERS

The truth of Christ's mystical body brings home to us not only that we are members of the Head, but also that we are members of one another (Rom 12:5). As a result we can see that holy communion not only binds us more closely to Christ but it also binds us more closely to our fellow members of Christ's body. The Eucharist is indeed a great privilege, but it also reveals a great responsibility. At the table of the Lord we must learn to be more aware of how we are members of other people and they of us. That means that they depend on us before God as we do on them. We need to pray for them, to offer ourselves to our Lord on their behalf and renew our commitment to that Christian vocation which calls on us to be "men and women for others".

⚡ 28 ⚡
INTERCOMMUNION

One of the great joys of the Church ever since the Second Vatican Council has been the growth in ecumenism among the Churches and the consequent development of relationships, both religious and social, among Christians generally. We seem to be witnessing an answer to the Lord's petition "that they may be one" (Jn 17:11). But among all this flourishing of Christian brotherhood there is one great cloud of sadness which has not yet lifted from the life of the Churches. It is the fact that Christians, who share a common Baptism, are not yet able to share a common Eucharist, even though the Eucharist is the great sacrament of Christian unity.

DIFFICULTIES ON THE WAY

In the gospels Jesus loves everyone and wants to be their food, so why not welcome everyone to our Eucharist? While this is true of our Lord's ultimate design for everyone, he was always a realist, and at times we find him making distinctions between people and postponing his graces in the case of those who are not yet ready for them. The soil must first be prepared before the seed can fall and take root (cf. Mt 13:4-9). If you are not yet properly reconciled, he says, go and be reconciled first; then come and offer your gift (Mt 5:23f). All the sacraments are sacraments of faith; that means that without due faith on the part of those who receive them, they simply do not work.

One of the reasons why many find all this hard to understand is the way we tend to put the individual first, whereas, in the gospel and in the Christian tradition, first comes the community of faith in which we come to belief. For too many of us our prayer and worship is still a matter of "Me and my Jesus", but that is not the way of the sacraments. The Eucharist is Christ nourishing his body, namely the Church. Our Lord loves us individually but not separately. As a result it is in feeding the Church that he feeds us individually.

THE MEANING OF THE SIGN

There is a great mystery here, namely that by which Christ is one with his Church. In John's gospel our Lord sees us as branches of the Vine (Jn 15:5); for St. Paul we are members of Christ's body (1 Rom 12:4f). Now the Eucharist is the highest sign of unity we have. That means that the full Eucharist (Mass with holy communion) is a sign of the fullness of the Church, and so a sign of our belonging to the Church from which we receive our union with Christ. If people are not yet full members of this Church, sharing its faith – if for instance they are not yet reconciled to the Pope as Vicar of Christ – then what the sacrament proclaims is not yet fully true of them and so, regrettably, they do not yet belong to this table with us.

In ecumenical relations the important thing is to find a sign that expresses the degree of unity we already have. This may lie in a common celebration of the Word of God, but it can also be found in a celebration of Mass together where those who do not receive communion come up for a blessing instead. To go to Mass without receiving communion was once a common practice among good Catholics. The practice can find a new meaning and usefulness in the circumstance we are describing.

⤳ 29 ⤶
A HEAVENLY REALITY

"Unless you eat the flesh of the Son of Man and drink his blood, you shall not have life in you" (Jn 6:53). When our Lord spoke those words in the synagogue at Capernaum, a shock-wave spread through the people. "How can this man give us his flesh to eat?" they asked. It sounded like cannibalism, and nothing could be more revolting than that. Perhaps our Lord was being deliberately provocative, separating the sheep from the goats, but the scandal his words created is still felt by people even today. The reaction of those who first heard these words is understandable enough, but the people who continue to be scandalized are certainly missing something. They have left out of account the mystery of the resurrection as well as the spiritual nature of holy communion.

THE RISEN CHRIST

Going to communion is above all a spiritual event. The physical act of eating the sacrament is simply a way of coming into union with the Lord, but that union is primarily a spiritual union, spirit to spirit, soul to soul, heart to heart. When we speak of the reality of Christ in the Eucharist, it is the risen Christ we have in mind, and that makes all the difference.

St Paul is very clear about the difference between a body in this life and a risen body (1 Cor 15:35-49). It is like the seed that falls into the ground; first it must die away before the new crop rises from the earth. What you sow, says St Paul, is not the same as the body it is going to be. From that which was buried in the ground something very different rises. Similarly in the resurrection of the dead. What is placed in the grave is weak and perishable; what rises is a new creation, glorious and immortal. What is buried is a natural body; when it rises from the dead it has been changed into "a spiritual body" (1 Cor 15:44); it is the spiritual reality of a person totally transformed, body and soul, into a heavenly being.

How all this comes about, of course, remains a great mystery. Just as the natural body buried in the grave has to be transformed into a spiritual and immortal reality, so our bread and wine, as mere natural things, have to be transformed into a heavenly reality before they can bring us all the graces of the sacrament. For the ordinary Christian, however, the "how" does not matter. What matters is the fact, as proclaimed in every Mass by our Lord himself, "This is my body...This is my blood," – and, as Peter said long ago, "Lord to whom shall we go? You have the words of eternal life" (Jn 6:69).

At the end of time, when the faithful departed rise from the grave, all that Paul has promised will become true in their case. In the meantime it is already true in the case of Christ, ever since he rose from the dead as "the first fruits of them that sleep" (1 Cor 15:20). This then is the heavenly reality we meet in the Eucharist, summoning us beyond natural things like bread and wine and even beyond his butchered flesh and blood as they were on Calvary. In the sacrament, in either host or chalice, the risen Christ, whole and entire, spiritual and transformed, is waiting to meet us, body, blood, soul and divinity. Taking into ourselves the body of Christ in his glory, we receive the pledge of one day sharing that glory with him in heaven.

⚮ 30 ⚮
SILENCE

Active participation in the liturgy was the great rallying-cry of Vatican II for the renewal of the liturgy. This has led to the present situation where plenty of hymns, mini-homilies throughout the Mass, movement and gesture of all kinds are the order of the day. Doubtless many of us have still a long way to go in that regard, but sometimes people can carry things too far. A common criticism of many liturgies is that there is too much talk. Words, words and more words can be a hindrance rather than a help. Liturgists can be in danger of making a mistake similar to that of the busy Martha, rather than learning from the contemplative Mary (Lk 10:38-42).

During his visit to Britain in 2010, Pope Benedict impressed many by the way he celebrated the liturgy. One of the surprising aspects of those liturgies was the use of silence. The Holy Father kept a notable period of silence after the homily and after holy communion. Then there was the dramatic spectacle of 95,000 people in Hyde Park in silent adoration of the Blessed Sacrament. Many people watching that scene at home on their television-sets felt moved to stop what they were doing and to share in that moment. Afterwards many remarked that for them this was the most moving part of the entire visit. "Be still and know that I am God," said the Psalmist (Ps 45:10).

TEACHING OF VATICAN II

This use of silence, of course, is not something new. It is recommended by the Vatican Council itself. Indeed, by a certain irony, when the council comes to list the various forms of active participation, it includes among them the use of silence. "At the proper times all should observe a reverent silence" (*Liturgy Constitution*, 30). The two main occasions for such silence in the course of the Mass are those observed by Pope Benedict, after the homily and after holy communion.

But how can such a silence be a form of active participation? It is because such moments are not empty of meaning. First of all, they can be filled with reverence, something we sometimes miss in our modern liturgies. Furthermore, as the Pope's Masses showed us, they can give us a sense of deep communion with God and with one another. In an exhortation to religious in 1971, Pope Paul VI spoke of the link between silence and prayer: "Faith, hope and a love of God which is open to the gifts of the Spirit, and also a brotherly love which is open to the mystery of others, carry with them an imperative need for silence."

THE BISHOPS OF IRELAND

In their recent edition of the *General Instruction of the Roman Missal* (Dublin: Veritas, 2005) the Irish Bishops recommend the same two periods of silence, while not making them obligatory. They also have something to say about silence in church generally. Before the Vatican Council it was normal for people to keep silent before and after the liturgy in order to let people pray. This principle was weakened somewhat during the confused years that followed the council. On this development the bishops have this to say (art. 45): "Even before the celebration itself it is commendable that silence be observed in church ... so that all may dispose themselves to carry out the sacred action in a devout and fitting manner."

⚘ 31 ⚘
THANKSGIVING AFTER COMMUNION

One of the unforgettable stories in the gospels is the one about the cure of the ten lepers (Lk 17:11-19). Only one of them came back to thank our Lord and he was a Samaritan. What surprises us most in this story is the depth of our Lord's feeling at being taken for granted by those who never took the trouble to return and thank him. From this we see that thanksgiving matters to God as well as to you and to me. That is something we should remember at Mass, since the Mass itself is one great act of thanksgiving to God. However there is one special gift which we receive at Mass which calls for special gratitude on our part, namely the very personal visit we receive from our Lord when he comes to us in holy communion.

The brief period after receiving the sacrament has long been seen in the Church as a moment of special grace. It is a time for intimate and personal conversation with our loving Saviour. This is something we have been taught from childhood on, and this ancient tradition has continued after Vatican II. Only a few years ago John Paul II spoke of "the intimate converse with Jesus which takes place after receiving communion" (*Ecclesia de Eucharistia*, art. 61).

The point was raised in a number of the official guidelines for the liturgy which came out after Vatican II. One of the first and most influential of these spoke as follows: "In order to remain more easily in this thanksgiving which is offered to God in an eminent way in the Mass, those who have been nourished by holy communion should be encouraged to remain for a while in prayer." A later guideline was even clearer: "The faithful are to be recommended not to omit a proper thanksgiving after communion. They may do this during the celebration, with a period of silence, with a hymn, psalm or other song of praise, or also after the celebration, if possible by staying behind to pray for a suitable time."

AN IMPORTANT CUSTOM

This practice is important for a number of reasons. The first and most obvious reason is the lesson we learn from the story of the ten lepers. It is simply a question of thanksgiving, and thanksgiving is something our Lord appreciates so much. The person who is ungrateful in ordinary things is somehow lacking in common humanity, but how much more pressing is the need to express our thanks when we receive such an unspeakable gift from Almighty God himself!

Then there is a question about how sacraments work. All the sacraments are "sacraments of faith" (Vatican II, *Liturgy Constitution*, art. 59). This means that they are not magic. They cannot bear fruit in our lives unless we receive them with faith – and the deeper and more heartfelt our faith, the more fruitful the sacraments will be within us. The prayer of faith after holy communion helps to deepen the fruitfulness of the sacrament in our lives.

From An Early Age

The issue we are discussing is especially important for parents and teachers responsible for bringing young children to holy communion. The children need to be trained from an early age in this practice of making a person-to-person, heart-to heart response to our Lord's coming to them in the sacrament. In the modern liturgy there is so much attention paid to a communal response to the Mass that the habit of personal individual response can easily be forgotten. The children need to be taught some prayers to say, for instance the familiar ones of St. Pius X once found in many prayer-books.

PART 5:
EUCHARISTIC OUTREACH

～ 32 ～
JOHN PAUL AND THE EUCHARIST

Many people, even today, will remember the extraordinary scenes in St. Peter's Square in Rome which we saw on our televisions screens at the time of the death of Pope John Paul II. In particular I recall the placards asking for his recognition as a saint straightaway – "Santo subito" in Italian. One of the great failures of the Irish media, both at that time and since, has been their slowness in appreciating the unique impact of this man on ordinary people throughout the world, and that not only among Christians. Like all of us, he had his shortcomings, but that cannot take away from the overwhelming impression on people of faith everywhere that this was a man of God.

HIS PERSONAL DEVOTION
We know from his life and preaching that a major source of inspiration and of strength for his personal life of faith was his devotion to the Eucharist. Not only is that revealed in the teaching documents he gave us, but it is clear from his personal practice as well. The Ursuline nuns in Warsaw tell the story of a young priest calling at their door one day in 1958. When asked if he could pray in

their chapel, they of course showed him in. After a time they looked in and found him prostrate before the Blessed Sacrament. Several hours later they came along to offer him supper, but he declined, saying that he would remain where he was until he had to catch his train sometime after midnight. That was the young Karol Woytila, the future Pope. Earlier that day Cardinal Wyszynski had informed him that the Pope had just appointed him auxiliary bishop of Krakow.

In the course of his time on the chair of Peter, Pope John Paul issued many memorable encyclicals on the various problems of the day, but in the eyes of many his most heartfelt encyclical was his final one, that on the Eucharist, *Ecclesia de Eucharistia*. Here the central message is that the Catholic Church is a Eucharistic Church; the heart of the Church is the Eucharist, and its life is a life lived from the Eucharist.

POINTS FROM THE ENCYCLICAL

This is a subject especially close to John Paul. In the encyclical he tells us that he wants the Eucharist to "continue to shine forth in all its radiant mystery" (art. 10). He writes first of the sacrifice of the Mass. Christ's love for us in his sacrifice, his "laying down his life for his friends" (Jn 15:13), becomes present for us with his sacrifice in the Eucharist. "What more could Jesus have done for us?" he asks. "Truly in the Eucharist he shows us a love which goes 'to the end' (Jn 13:1), a love which knows no measure" (art. 11).

Then he writes of the mystery of presence. The Eucharist is "the gift *par excellence*, for it is the gift of himself, of his person in his sacred humanity as well as the gift of his saving work" (art. 11). No wonder he is concerned about "shadows" over Eucharistic teaching leading to the confusion of the faithful. "The Eucharist is too great a gift to tolerate ambiguity and depreciation" (art. 10).

For many the most memorable section of the encyclical speaks of the Pope's personal devotion to the Blessed Sacrament. We have already seen evidence of that devotion in the story from the Ursulines of Warsaw. In the encyclical he speaks of it from the heart. The daily practice of prayer before the Blessed Sacrament, he tells us, "becomes an inexhaustible source of holiness" (art. 10). Then he recounts his personal experience of this practice. "It is pleasant to spend time with him, to lie close to his breast like the Beloved Disciple and to feel the infinite love present in his heart ... How often, dear brothers and sisters, have I not experienced this, and drawn from it strength, consolation and support" (art. 25).

⇜ 33 ⇝
REST-STOP FOR THE SOUL

Service-stations are a familiar sight on the great motorways of Europe where one can turn aside for re-fuelling or a sandwich. There is one country however, Germany, where the service-stations often include a church, offering the weary driver the opportunity for a few moments peace and quiet and prayer. Many of these "Motorway Churches", as they are called, keep a Visitors' Book, where weary road-users can record their thoughts and prayers as they go on their journey.

FROM THE VISITOR'S BOOK

A programme on the B.B.C. recently reported on some of these messages to give us an insight into what these special chapels of reflection can mean for people. Commonly there are petitions like this one, "Please God, help me to drive slowly in my new Audi. Drive with me so that nothing bad happens." Then there are acts of thanksgiving: "I am here because I have just come so close to having an accident. I am so grateful I didn't crash." Another man wrote out of an anguished reflection on his life: "Dear God, please let my wife become the woman she used to be."

The most frequented Motorway-Church in all Germany is St. Christopher's in Bavaria, in the care of the local Catholic priest and situated on the busy road between Munich and Berlin. There the B.B.C. journalist ran into a number of reflective people. One was the head of a textile-firm, driving 50,000 miles a year. He remarked that in life power comes from silence; and coming into the quiet of St. Christopher's gives him the power to get on with life and with his business.

A busy medical doctor said, "It is hard work treating sick people all day long, so it is good to have five minutes peace for myself in the church." The managing-director of a factory said, "In my life I have to fight for everything. The construction-business is an angry business, but I must also fight to stay a human being. That is why I come here. It gives me a good feeling – a good feeling for my soul." One proprietor of a service-station put it this way: we need rest-stops for the body, hence our restaurant; we need rest-stops for the car, hence our garage; and we need rest-stops for the soul, hence the church.

EMMANUEL – GOD WITH US

Not all these Motorway Churches are Catholic, but those which are have the added blessing of the Real Presence in the tabernacle. In the hectic pace of modern life we all need to learn this lesson from the busy movers and shakers of the economic power-house which is modern Germany. They help to remind us Catholics of the point about our ancient custom of visits to the Blessed Sacrament.

Before the tabernacle we will all be the better for a few moments quiet, reflection and prayer, recovering something of our own humanity from the human presence of our God who desires to be so close to us. The tabernacle is always a sign to us of our Lord's desire to be part of our everyday and to prolong his presence in our lives from one celebration of Mass to the next. We might read again the quotation from John Paul II with which the preceding chapter concluded.

～ 34 ～
COMMUNION OF THE SICK

One of the unforgettable images of Jesus in the New Testament is his ministry to the sick and dying. They came from all quarters of

Galilee, the lame, the blind, the lepers, and he tried to help them all. This was not just to prove something by the wonder of it. The main reason for it all was simply the compassion in the heart of God which went out to them all.

A LONG HISTORY

In the course of time it was inevitable that Christians should seek similar help and strength from the Saviour who lives on in the sacraments, and one of the main expressions of that continuing ministry of Jesus is the custom of bringing communion to the sick. Indeed this is one of the first things we learn about the sacrament in the early Church: they liked to bring holy communion to the sick in their homes. St Justin, who was martyred in the middle of the second century, tells us about it, and so it has continued down to our own day, though the accompanying ceremonies and customs have varied over the centuries.

One of the great changes introduced in our own times has been the opening up to lay men and women of the ministry of bringing the sacrament to the sick. This in fact marks a return to the practice of the early centuries when Christian men and women commonly brought communion to their own homes, to the sick and to those in prison.

TWO POINTS OF DOCTRINE

There are two important points about the Eucharist which are implied by this practice. The first is that it underlines how our Lord's presence in the host is a continuing presence. It does not end when the Mass ends but only when the host is consumed.

Secondly, the practice underlines the link between communion and the Mass. The purpose of the consecration of the sacrament during the Eucharistic Prayer is to draw every communicant into a deeper union with Christ's offering of himself which we celebrate in the Eucharistic Prayer. This applies, of course, to those who go to communion during the Mass, but it has a special relevance for the sick who cannot take part in the Mass directly. It helps them to unite their sufferings with those of Christ and to offer them to God in union with the offering which Christ makes in every Mass.

THE CARE OF THE SICK

Ever since our Lord showed his concern for those who are ill, the trials of the sick have had a special meaning for the Church. This is reflected in the official document dealing with the matter, *The Pastoral Care of the Sick*. In this instruction the Church explains how holy communion brings a new value to the trials and difficulties of those who are ill. The sacrament does this by uniting them more deeply with Christ in his struggle with evil, in his prayer for the world and in his love for the Father (art. 73).

One of the common difficulties of those who are house-bound as a result of sickness or old age is loneliness. The Church is conscious of this too, for it reminds us that the communion of the sick reunites them with the Eucharistic community from which illness has separated them (art. 51).

FOOD FOR THE JOURNEY

Communion of the sick has a special meaning for the person who is drawing near to death. After Vatican II the Church reformed its ritual of anointing. This is no longer seen as the last sacrament before death. That is why the name was changed from "Extreme Unction" to "the Sacrament of the Sick", and it is to be administered at the onset of any serious illness, whether a person is close to death or not.

As the last hours draw near however, a person can often still be well enough to receive holy communion. In this case the sacrament is called "viaticum", which means "food for the journey". Christians see it as a special sign of God's mercy to the dying person and a singular consolation to those about to be bereaved by the passing of the one they love. It is the believer's last act of participation in the mystery celebrated in the Eucharist, namely the mystery of the death of the Lord and of his passage to the Father (art. 175). In line with this the Church describes Viaticum as the sacrament of the passage through death to eternal life (art. 26).

EUCHARIST AND ART

One day in 1868 a young boy from near Ardagh in Co. Limerick went out hunting rabbits. What he found that day far surpassed his expectations. He stumbled on one of the greatest treasures of Irish art, what we now call the Ardagh Chalice. This masterpiece of the craft of Irish gold and silversmiths had lain in the soil for a thousand years, probably concealed when the Vikings were terrorizing the land. It seems to date from the eighth century and can be seen in the National Museum in Dublin.

This period in Ireland was one of the most creative times in our history. The artistry of the Ardagh Chalice is matched by another great relic from those early centuries, the Book of Kells. This book is associated with the great monastery of the monks of Colmcille in Kells, Co. Meath. After the destruction of the parent monastery in the Scottish island of Iona, Kells became the leading monastery for the sons of Colmcille, and this was their book of the gospels, inscribed with loving imagination and infinite attention to detail. The Annals of the Four Masters refer to it as "the great gospel of Colmcille" and "the chief treasure of the western world".

EVIDENCE OF FAITH

These two masterpieces of Irish art are not only proof of the creativity of our forbears. They are eloquent evidence of the faith that inspired them and in particular of the love of the Mass. Each of them in its own way points to one or other of the two main parts of the Mass, the Liturgy of the Word and the Liturgy of the Eucharist. The Book of Kells shows us that for these people of long ago only the most beautiful book in the world was worthy to be used in the Liturgy of the Word. The Ardagh Chalice shows us that only one of the most beautiful vessels in the world was worthy to hold the blood of Christ in the sacrament. Every jewel, every carefully incised line on this masterpiece reflects the faith of the people of the time in the Real Presence of our Lord in the Eucharist. One of them, the eighth century poet Blathmac, wrote as follows:

It is your Son's body that comes to us
When one goes to the sacrament;
The pure wine has been transmuted for us
Into the blood of the Son of the King.

THE GRANDEUR OF THE EVENT

To this day the feeling is strong in the Church that the Mass should take place in a setting of beauty. Vatican II tells us that "all things set apart for use in divine worship should be worthy, becoming and beautiful, signs and symbols of things supernatural" (*Liturgy Constitution*, 122). In his encyclical on the Eucharist, John Paul II had the same message. Having recalled the care with which the apostles prepared the Upper Room for the Last Supper (Mk 14:15), he pointed out that the faith of the Church not only requires us to come to Mass with inner devotion but also "in outward forms meant to evoke and emphasize the grandeur of the event being celebrated" (*Ecclesia de Eucharistia*, 49).

The Holy Father goes on to speak of the rich artistic heritage which has developed around the Eucharist. "Architecture, sculpture, painting and music, moved by the Christian mystery, have found in the Eucharist, both directly and indirectly, a source of great inspiration" (ibid.). We have only to recall some of the great masterpieces of European art to see the truth of that remark. Beauty evokes beauty; and the beauty of what the Lord did for us in the Eucharist should evoke beauty in all that we bring to the Mass. In this, as in so many other ways, the spiritual wisdom of our ancestors in the faith has shown us the way.

～ 36 ～
MARY AND THE EUCHARIST

Mary is "the woman of the Eucharist". This phrase comes from the pen of Pope John Paul II in his encyclical, *Ecclesia de Eucharistia*, from which the quotations given below are taken. In the final chapter of this encyclical he wished to honour the special relationship that exists between the Mother of God and the great sacrament given to us by her Son. This message was to be part of the Holy Father's special legacy to the Church.

MOTHER OF THE EUCHARIST

The word *eucharist* means thanksgiving, and as the liturgy itself says, it is our duty and our salvation always and everywhere to give God thanks. In the story of the Visitation a great prayer of thanksgiving is placed upon the lips of Mary which we call the *Magnificat*. As a result of this prayer Mary is for us a model of the spirit of praise and thanksgiving for the great things the Lord has done (Lk 2:46-55). Indeed because of the depth of love and heartfelt gratitude revealed to us in the heart of Mary, she has become not only Mother of the Church but also Mother of the Eucharist, pointing to gratitude as the way to enter into the mystery of this sacrifice.

Commonly the great things of God come only at a price, and in Mary's case Simeon foretold how a sword would pierce her heart (Lk 2:34f). The Holy Father reflects how, ever since those words of Simeon, Mary was preparing for Calvary every day by the spirit of self-offering to God which she always carried in her heart. Finally it all comes to a high point at the foot of the cross in the unforgettable mystery of her union with her Son in his passion. The apostle John was rewarded for his fidelity when our dying Saviour gave him Mary as his mother, and, as the Holy Father puts it, he does the same for each of us in every Eucharist.

THE BODY OF CHRIST

Pope John Paul goes on to reflect on the mystery of the body of Christ in the Eucharist: "The body given up for us and made present under sacramental signs was the same body which she had conceived in her womb" (art. 56). Mary was asked to believe that her son was the Son of God. In continuity with Mary's faith we are asked to believe that the same Jesus Christ becomes present to us under the signs of bread and wine.

In bearing the physical reality of her Son for nine months in her womb Mary anticipated what to some degree happens sacramentally in every believer who receives the Lord in the Eucharist. What an experience it must have been for Mary herself to receive holy communion from the apostles, "welcoming once more into her womb that heart which had beat in unison with hers" (art. 56).

CONTEMPLATION AND AMAZEMENT

There are two words which constantly keep returning to the pen of John Paul II, and each has a special meaning for the Eucharist and for Mary. The first of these is contemplation. Our Lady, of course, is one of the great models of contemplation in the New Testament, pondering all these mysteries in her heart (Lk 2:19 and 52). For the Holy Father a special object of contemplation is the mystery of the reserved sacrament (art. 25). He brings both of these aspects together when he sees Mary in the Visitation to Elizabeth as "the first tabernacle in history" (art. 55). Then he thinks of our contemplation: "Gazing on her we come to know the transforming power present in the Eucharist. In her we see the world renewed in love" (art. 62).

The second word is "amazement" which is one of the fruits of contemplation. The Holy Father likes to speak of "Eucharistic amazement" (art. 5f). When we recall what an extraordinary mystery the Eucharist is and how beautiful is Mary's role in bringing his body into the world, we cannot but be filled with amazement at the wonderful ways of God. Her amazement becomes a model for ours. The Holy Father reminds us of "the enraptured gaze of Mary as she contemplated the face of the newborn Christ and cradled him in her arms" (art. 55). This should be an inspiration to us just to spend time with our Lord in thanksgiving after holy communion or in quiet prayer and adoration before the Blessed Sacrament.

37

THE SACRED HEART AND THE EUCHARIST

During the Eucharistic congress in 1932 Dublin was covered in decorations. Across one of the poorer streets of the city there was a banner which said, "God bless the Sacred Heart." While some might be amused by the theology of that statement, they could easily miss the point of the genuine devotion it expressed. At that time one could almost say that Irish faith was defined by devotion to the Sacred Heart. The red lamp before the Sacred Heart picture in homes throughout the land said it all; and so people knew instinctively, from when they were knee-high, that Jesus was a God of love and compassion.

TWO FEAST-DAYS
There was even a theological point behind the banner which not everyone today grasps in the same instinctive way. Between the mystery of love in the Eucharist, being celebrated by the Eucharistic Congress, and the mystery of love summed up in the image of the Sacred Heart there is a profound and mysterious connection. It goes back in fact to the origin of our devotion to the Sacred Heart, when our Lord appeared to St. Margaret Mary (1647-1690) in her convent chapel in Paray-le-monial, France.

There, as she used to pray before the Blessed Sacrament, our Lord appeared to her in a series of apparitions under the form of the Sacred Heart, inviting the world to enter into this devotion. In the year 1675, during the octave of Corpus Christi, the feast of Christ's body and blood, there took place "the great apparition" in which our Lord asked that the feast of the Sacred Heart be held on the Friday after the end of the octave of Corpus Christi, and that is when we celebrate it to this day. The two feasts, Corpus Christi and the Feast of the Sacred Heart, belong together as two manifestations of the one divine mystery.

GIFT OF HIS HEART
The sacrament of the Eucharist is a gift of Christ's heart to the Church. There is an event at the conclusion of John's account of the Passion

which expresses that truth in a solemn and mysterious way (Jn 19:34-36). Towards the end of that dreadful day, when our Saviour was already dead on the cross, one of the soldiers opened his side with a lance, and there came out blood and water. The key word here is "opened", as St Augustine points out. This event is a prophetic sign of the opening up of the mystery of Christ's love in dying for us and of that love flowing out to all of us through the sacraments of the Church, especially the sacrament of Christ's body and blood. You have only to read the preface of the Mass of the Sacred Heart to see that this is the meaning which the Church finds in that event.

MYSTERIES OF LOVE

When one reflects on the meaning of the Sacred Heart and of the Eucharist, one can see that the two mysteries belong together in a profound way because both are about love, mercy and compassion. What above all else will move us to love our fellow human beings and to be forgiving and merciful towards them is the love that Christ shows to each one from the depths of that heart of his which is both fully human and fully divine. What above all else helps us to live up to that ideal and to grow in the virtues which it implies is the body and blood of our Saviour bestowed upon us in the mystery of the Eucharist.

38
TRINITY AND EUCHARIST

Some eighteen hundred years before Christ, the word of the Lord came to the patriarch Abraham. The Lord was calling him from his home in southern Iraq to journey into the unknown, ending up in Palestine. That journey took great faith, and Abraham is of course, as our liturgy calls him, "our father in faith."

It is always worth bearing in mind that the God who spoke to Abraham is the same God who is worshipped in the three great religions that look back to Abraham: Judaism, Christianity and Islam.

In a world where religious differences receive so much attention, it is always good to keep in mind the significant points we hold in common. The faith of Abraham is one of them, and from him we all believe that in some sense God the Creator is one God.

Though Islam was the last of the three religions to come about, it has more in common with Judaism than either Judaism or Islam has with Christianity. The point of difference, of course, is the person of Christ. Jews see Moses as a prophet, and Muslims see Mahomet as the greatest of the prophets, but for Christians Jesus is "more than a prophet". He is the Son of God himself, a second divine person "in whom dwells all the fullness of the divinity corporeally" (Col 2:9). This means that Christians have their own fundamentally different understanding of God even though it is the same God we all worship.

GOD IS CLOSE

For Christians God is no distant being in the heavens waiting to be worshipped across an infinite gulf. In his love and mercy for us God has bridged that gulf. Our God is the God who comes close. This in a nutshell is the point about the mystery of the Trinity.

God has come close to us, first of all, in the person of his Son, who came to walk this earth and share our history. Secondly, God comes close in the person of the Holy Spirit, the third divine person, who lives in our hearts if we remain in the state of grace. Furthermore, the Holy Spirit lives on in the Church to enable us, through the Church, to rediscover Christ, who continues to be present to us in his own way, especially through the sacraments.

THE DIVINE INDWELLING

This continuing presence of the Holy Spirit within us was promised to us by our Lord at the Last Supper as long as we remain friends of God: "He (the Holy Spirit) will be continually at your side, nay, he will be in you" (Jn 14:17, Knox Translation). Now one of the things the Holy Spirit does for us is to bring us the continuing presence of the Father and Son as well (Jn 14:23). This is the privilege of Christians who remain in the state of grace: to go through life with

Father, Son and Holy Spirit dwelling within them. Our God is a God who shares his life with us and shares himself with us.

The most profound and mysterious instance of that sharing is the Eucharist. Through our receiving our Lord in Holy Communion the divine persons reach into the depths of our being to strengthen our grasp of their presence within us. This is the supreme experience here below of that love of God for us by which he is not content to sit in heaven and receive our worship from afar. To each one going to communion we can apply those words of the Apocalypse, "Behold, I stand at the door and knock; if anyone hears my voice and opens the door, I will come to him and eat with him, and he with me" (Apoc 3:20).

PART 6:
THE EUCHARISTIC PRAYERS

～ 39 ～
INTRODUCING THE PRAYERS

A previous chapter in this book gave an account of that part of the Mass which we refer to as the canon or the Eucharistic Prayer. Up to the Second Vatican Council the Western Church had only one form of prayer at this section of the Mass. In the reform of the liturgy after Vatican II it was decided to widen our choice of prayer-form and to add alternative canons or Eucharistic Prayers to the ancient Roman Canon. While at present we have several such official prayers at our disposal, there are four main ones which must be found in every altar missal. In these concluding chapters we will look at each of these main Eucharistic Prayers in turn. Quotations from the prayers will be made both from the new (2011) translation and from the text with which we have been familiar since 1969.

We all know well the story in the gospels of how our Lord instituted the Eucharist at the Last Supper. In fact we have four different versions of what he said and did, each of them slightly different, but in all of them we hear of his "thanking" or "blessing" his Father before giving to the apostles the bread and cup. Here we see our Lord following the Jewish custom of prayers of blessing and thanksgiving before sharing their food at table. The exact form of our Lord's prayer of blessing and thanksgiving on that occasion is not known to us, but it followed the general pattern of Jewish prayer. That is the origin of our Eucharistic Prayers.

THE CHURCH'S LITURGY

When the Christian Church came to organise its worship in the early years, the question had to be raised as to what would be an appropriate form of words with which to accompany Christ's great act of worship in the Mass. The answer to that question seems to have come out of the rich tradition of prayer of the Jewish people, and most likely out of the kind of prayers they used over bread and wine when they said grace before and after meals. It is helpful to think of Eucharistic Prayers as growing our of Jewish table prayer. In time Christian Eucharistic Prayer went its own way, particularly by placing at the centre of our prayers our Lord's own words over the bread and wine at the Last Supper.

We will now examine the text of each of the four main Eucharistic Prayers, but before doing so it will be well to bear in mind that this part of the Mass is more than just offering a beautiful prayer to God. In the course of reciting these texts we are at the high point of the action of the Mass for which these prayers are the verbal accompaniment. The central action of the Mass is Christ's great act of worship of his Father. By celebrating the Eucharistic Prayer with the priest we identify ourselves with Christ's worship, offering our lives to God through, with and in his Son, by the power of the Holy Spirit. That is the fundamental event that occurs as these Eucharistic Prayers are celebrated by the Church gathered in worship.

MOVEMENTS OF PRAYER

To follow the Eucharistic Prayer and make it our own is a skill that has to be learnt. Prior to the Second Vatican Council the Eucharistic Prayer was mostly celebrated in silence and the people followed it in various ways of their own devotion. Nowadays they will need more help. Some knowledge of the text, such as that given in this book, can assist them. Particular help will be found in becoming familiar with the three basic movements of prayer described in the earlier chapter entitled "The Great Prayer". Here it is not so much a question of the words but of entering into the spirit of the relevant parts of the prayer and making these movements our own.

≈ 40 ≈
THE FIRST EUCHARISTIC PRAYER

The First Eucharistic Prayer is sometimes called the Roman Canon since it gives us the form in which this part of the Mass has been celebrated in the Church of Rome ever since the fourth century. We do not know who composed it, but we do know that it has been prayed down through the centuries by all the great saints of the western Church. Consequently it is a venerable prayer, not only by reason of its antiquity, but also by reason of the sanctity of all the generations who have prayed it. There is something awesome in taking on our lips a prayer which has been with the Church so long and has helped so many people to enter into the presence of God.

Of our four main Eucharistic Prayers this one is at once the longest and the most solemn. To appreciate the spirit of the prayer one should have in mind the great sacrifice of Christ as described in the Letter to the Hebrews, or the heavenly liturgy around the throne of God as described in the last book of the Bible, the Apocalypse.

NEW TESTAMENT BACKGROUND

In the Letter to the Hebrews we see clearly that Christ's sacrifice, like all Jewish sacrifices, was carried out in two stages. First of all there is the immolation of the victim, which in the case of Christ took place once for all on the cross. Then there is the consummation of the sacrifice as the body and blood of the victim are brought to the altar to deepen the union between God and the people. In Christ's case the altar, of course, is in heaven, where the risen and glorified Christ makes intercession for us for all time.

This scene from the Letter to the Hebrews is the back-drop for the great act of worship which is expressed in the First Eucharistic Prayer. Offering and intercession are two major themes running through the First Eucharistic Prayer, linking our worship here on earth with that victorious intercession of our great High Priest in heaven and his continuous offering of his sacrifice to his Father on our behalf.

Then there is the account of heaven in the book of the Apocalypse. In chapters 4 to 7 of this book we are given a vision of the heavenly liturgy. There we see all the various ranks of angels and saints gathered around the throne of God and the Lamb, the patriarchs, the apostles and the martyrs, "all in heaven and on earth and under the earth" (Apoc 5:13) praising and thanking God., with the angels offering up the incense of the prayers of the saints (Apoc 5:8).

This is the setting for all the intercessions in the First Eucharistic Prayer as it goes through the various ranks of the People of God. Here we commemorate the saints in heaven, the leaders of the Church on earth, the Pope and the bishops and those "under the earth", namely the faithful departed. The ancient and eloquent prayer for the dead in the First Eucharistic Prayer is the most beautiful expression of this theme in all our Eucharistic Prayers.

A ROMAN STRUCTURE

Finally we might notice how all this wealth of faith and affection is drawn together into a careful structure, in the spirit of the Roman sense of order. It has been compared to the structure of one of those ancient Roman basilicas.

Before and after the consecration at the centre of the canon there are corresponding passages of prayer balancing each other, for instance the lists of apostles and their successors balancing the list of martyrs; the memento of the living balancing the memento of the dead; the prayer of praise in the Preface balancing the magnificent "Through him, and with him, and in him..." with which this canon reaches its climax. This final passage of prayer (called the Doxology) is so striking that it has been borrowed from the First Eucharistic Prayer to form the conclusion of all our Eucharistic Prayers.

THE SECOND EUCHARISTIC PRAYER

You will have heard of the catacombs of Rome. The term refers to the mazes of underground galleries, still surviving, where the early Christians used to bury their dead. At points where galleries converge there are more open spaces, and there the Christians sometimes gathered for the celebration of the Eucharist. At the time of the Second Vatican Council many people were speaking and writing of the Church of the Catacombs, looking back for inspiration to the simplicity and courage of those Christians of long ago. In their day those Roman Christians were a persecuted minority, mostly poor, and many of them destined to die as martyrs.

THE CANON OF HIPPOLYTUS
One part of the liturgy of the catacombs that has come down to us is an ancient Eucharistic Prayer, which dates from the early third century and is known as the Canon of Hippolytus. Its composition is commonly attributed to a priest of that name who was martyred in Rome in the early third century and whose feast is on August 13th. This prayer is particularly precious to us, since it gives unique testimony to the faith and spirituality of the Church of those early martyrs.

When the decision was made at the time of Vatican II to add new Eucharistic Prayers to the traditional Roman Canon, people thought first of the Canon of Hippolytus as a model for such a new prayer. The text of Hippolytus had to be modified somewhat, but eventually the liturgists gave us the Second Eucharistic Prayer, which draws the main part of its language from the ancient Roman prayer. The history of its origin gives us a clue for appreciating not only the language but the spirit of the new prayer.

The Second Eucharistic Prayer is the shortest of our four main prayers, its simplicity recalling that of the Church of the Catacombs. As with many of the great Eucharistic Prayers of the Eastern Church, the Preface is an integral part of what has come down to us. Indeed the text of Hippolytus begins before the Preface with the familiar dialogue between priest and people where we are asked to lift up our hearts. It is good to know that this dialogue is that ancient and in fact goes back to a Jewish custom of introducing prayers of thanksgiving with a somewhat similar dialogue.

The first thing that strikes us about this prayer is that it is a proclamation of the mighty deeds of God in salvation history. This is a frequent theme in the tradition of Eucharistic Prayers, with its roots in some of the great prayers of the Old Testament, thanking God for the gift of the covenant. In Hippolytus however the focus is on the New Testament, and the prayer celebrates the great deeds of God in the story of Christ, his incarnation, his passion and the gift of the Holy Spirit.

THE KING OF MARTYRS

However the most striking feature of this prayer arises from its background in the Church of the Martyrs. Its spirituality is that of the martyrs and its focus is the achievement of Christ as the King of Martyrs. Part of the mystery of the martyrs' death is their freedom in their dying. Here we celebrate the sovereign freedom of Christ in the face of death, "a death he freely accepted", or as the new missal has it, he "entered willingly into his death."

This same mystery is present in the way the love of Christ on the cross turned death into life and defeat into victory. Thus our Lord, in his freedom, opens his arms on the cross and, like the suffering Saviour in the fourth gospel, already in the midst of the passion he reveals or manifests the resurrection. In a sense the resurrection begins on the cross, since our Lord rises above his sufferings by accepting them from his Father and offering them up in freedom for the salvation of the world.

Finally we might notice the mention of the Holy Spirit in the Second Eucharistic Prayer. We easily take that for granted nowadays, but in fact, prior to Vatican II, it was not clear in the tradition of Western Eucharistic Prayer. However there was a clear petition for the coming of the Holy Spirit in Hippolytus' prayer, and that example helped the liturgists of Vatican II to include such a petition in all our new Eucharistic Prayers. As a result one of the great achievements of the new liturgy flowing from Vatican II has been a growing awareness among the faithful of the role of the Holy Spirit in our lives of faith.

◦ 42 ◦
THE THIRD EUCHARISTIC PRAYER

When the leaders of the Church gathered for the Second Vatican Council they were very conscious of the need to "read the signs of the times" and to interpret them in the light of the gospel (*Constitution on the Church in the World*, art. 4). As the work of the council came to be summed up in the new liturgy, it was only appropriate that this concern should pass into the prayer of the Church generally, and into the Eucharistic Prayer in particular.

One of the fundamental needs in the hearts of people today is found in their desire for unity and community on all the different levels of social life (*Constitution on the Church in the World*, art. 32). Since this desire fits in with one of the basic themes of the gospel, it was clear that this could most appropriately figure as a theme of Eucharistic Prayer; and that is what we have in the Third Eucharistic Prayer.

ONE BODY, ONE PEOPLE

The concern for unity was a theme dear to the council. It was evident not only in the teaching on ecumenism but also even in the council's notion of the Church itself. In the Third Eucharistic Prayer this note of unity is struck already in the opening address to God, as expressed in the new translation: "You never cease to gather a people to yourself, so that from the rising of the sun to its setting a pure sacrifice may be offered to your name." Later in the prayer we see that one of the main fruits of the celebration will be that we become "one body, one spirit in Christ". Finally we ask Almighty God that he may "gather to yourself all your children scattered throughout the world."

The Constitution on the Church devotes the whole of its seventh chapter to the Church as "the pilgrim people". This idea is echoed in this prayer when it speaks of "your pilgrim Church on earth". Here we might notice a certain contrast between the first and the third of our Eucharistic Prayers. The Roman Canon celebrates the Church largely as fully formed in its glorified state in heaven. The Third Eucharistic Prayer focuses more on the Church as a people in the process of being formed here on earth through the ups and downs of history.

THE ROLE OF THE SPIRIT

Traditionally the theme of unity is especially associated with the work of the Holy Spirit, and so it was only to be expected that the role of the Spirit should be explicit in this prayer. Already at the beginning of the prayer we hear that all life and grace flowing from the Father and from Christ come to us "by the power and working of the Holy Spirit". This principle is then applied to our petition that bread and wine become Christ's body and blood, for it is by the power of this same Spirit that this change is to come about.

After the consecration we come to one of the most striking expressions in the prayer. It is usual in such canons to pray that the sacrament bear fruit within us. Few canons express this theme in as memorable a manner as the Third Eucharistic Prayer. We pray that we may be filled with the Holy Spirit and "become one body, one spirit in Christ". In the tradition of the Church the Holy Spirit is "the soul" of the body of Christ. As a result we can say that this gift of the Spirit helps to build up the unity of the body of Christ. A concern for unity, as we have seen, is one of the great issues of modern life generally. By making this concern its own in the manner we have described the Vatican Council and its liturgy were clearly responding in their own way to the signs of the times.

THE FOURTH EUCHARISTIC PRAYER

This canon brings us to a different world. Here the new liturgy turns to the Church of the East and draws on the rich traditions of faith and spirituality to be found there. The main model chosen for what eventually became the Fourth Eucharistic Prayer was an ancient prayer associated with St. Basil, the great champion of the doctrine of the Trinity (c.330–379).

SALVATION HISTORY

The celebration of salvation history has long been a favourite theme of Eastern Eucharistic prayer. Such prayers are somewhat like a creed, going through the great events of the past which bear witness to God's providence over his people. This history has its ultimate climax in the coming of God's kingdom at the end of time, but before coming to that high point, the story of salvation follows the people of God through the great moments of their history. This story is revealed to us in the bible and is summed up for us in the section of this prayer that comes after the Holy, Holy, Holy, where the text of the prayer brings before us the whole sweep of salvation history. With history coming after the preface, the preface itself is pre-historical, focussed on creation and on the creator himself, who lives, we are told, "in unapproachable light".

Here we might reflect on another aspect of the mystery of God which underlies this canon. The doctrine of the Trinity has often sounded very unreal and distant to the ordinary faithful. However this doctrine is not talking about God as though he were a million miles away. In fact, as the chapter on "Trinity and Eucharist" above made clear, this teaching is about how God in his love has drawn close to us. In line with this way of thinking we can see this Eucharistic Prayer as celebrating how God in a sense has unfolded himself and entered into history in order to embrace us and draw us to himself. This he does especially through the gift of the Eucharist and through the gift of the Holy Spirit, drawing our ordinary lives, as the old translation has it, into "the one body of Christ, a living sacrifice of praise".

THE TASKS OF THE SPIRIT

Of particular interest in this prayer is the way it speaks of the third person of the Trinity. The role of the Holy Spirit was always a special feature of Eastern prayer. As this canon is so dependent on the Eastern tradition, this seems an appropriate place in which to bring out the Eucharistic role of the Spirit, and specifically the two main tasks here attributed to him, though in fact these are now found in all our new prayers.

The two tasks of the Spirit are expressed in two petitions that we make to God. In the first of these, which in our prayers comes before the consecration, we ask that the Holy Spirit may change our bread and wine into the body and blood of Christ. This is indeed an extraordinary petition, but it is only a prelude to the second petition which is made after the consecration. In this we are looking to the fulfilment of the whole plan of God for the Eucharist: we ask that our participation in the sacrament may deepen our profound communion with God and with one another.

The union that we seek here is no simple growth in a feeling of brotherly love and togetherness. What the Church desires and prays for is that we enter more deeply into that great mystery of our union in the body of Christ. For such a divine grace we need nothing less that the divine gift of the sacrament. We pray that our bread and wine be changed into such a gift in order that we in turn may be changed and so become more truly members of one another or, as some put it, become Christ for each other. Placing this profound pattern of change under the patronage of the Holy Spirit, the new Eucharistic Prayers illustrate in a concrete way the general role of the Holy Spirit which is well described by the Fourth Eucharistic Prayer as bringing to completion or perfection the work of Christ in the world.

PART 7:
CONCLUSION

ᵉ⁹ 44 ᵉ⁹
THE HEART OF THE MATTER

In this book we have seen something of the wealth of meaning and history which is to be found in our familiar celebration of the Mass, in its rituals, its truths and its implications for human living. In the midst of such diversity one always runs the risk of missing the wood for the trees; so here at the end of our reflections it seems a good idea to consider whether there is any one aspect which stands out above all others and is indeed the heart of the matter. It seems to this writer that there is, namely one's friendship with Christ.

WHAT THINK YOU OF CHRIST?
When all is said and done, Christianity is about Christ and our personal relationship with him. It is not about a law (as the Jews believe), nor about a book (as the Muslims believe), but about a person. One of the central questions which the gospels put to us is that once put to the Pharisees by our Lord himself, "What think you of Christ?" (Mt 22:42).

When we consider all the people we meet in life, all the people who put themselves forward for our attention or allegiance, indeed when we think of all the characters of history who claim our admiration or enthusiasm, they fade into insignificance when set beside the man from Nazareth, the Good Shepherd, the Captain of our souls. St. Paul left us in no doubt where he stood: "Furthermore I count all things as so much waste when compared with the excellent knowledge of Jesus Christ my Lord, for whom I have suffered the loss of all things, and I count them all as dung if only I can have Christ" (Phil 3:8).

For Christians there is one thing that matters above all others and that is our friendship with Christ. Most of us come to this friendship in childhood. We learn to talk to Jesus, to ask him for the things that matter to us, to trust him when he gives us something else. To him we bring our sorrows and our joys, knowing that if it is important to us it is important to him, for even the very hairs of your head are counted by him (Mt 10:30).

For parents and teachers there is no more wonderful task than to bring young minds and hearts into this friendship, to explain it to them, to help them to grow in it and to deepen it in their lives. In doing that we are giving them something that will stay with them forever, even into the next life.

THE SEAL ON OUR FRIENDSHIP

The Eucharist is the seal on our friendship with Christ. It is the doorway through which we go to meet him and he comes to us. It is the nourishment which helps that friendship to grow. He himself has given us the Eucharist as the means for that friendship to remain strong in our lives, to grow and to deepen. Some people might desire to be friends of Christ without taking the trouble to go to Mass, but we can hardly claim to be true to that friendship if we turn our backs on the means that he himself has given us for expressing our friendship and deepening it.

Every Sunday he stands at the door and knocks (Apoc 3:20). He invites us to join him in his own friendship with his Father and in his worship of him: "Do this in memory of me" (Lk 22:19). He sits us down at table with himself, and there he serves us and eats with us, and we with him (Lk 12:37; Apoc 3:20). In this celebration of the Christian sacrament we already anticipate something of what our friendship with Christ will be when it comes to its full flowering in the kingdom of heaven. In the long run that is all that matters.